KING*f*ISHER

First
Encyclopedia
of the
Human Body

First
Encyclopedia
of the
Human Body

Richard Walker

KING*f*ISHER

Editors Julie Ferris, Jonathan Stroud

Designer Malcolm Parchment

Consultant Dr Roy Palmer

Photography Geoff Dann, Tim Ridley

Illustrations Alan Hancock, Guy Smith, Gina Suter

Picture Research Manager Jane Lambert

DTP Co-ordinator Nicky Studdart

Production Controller Richard Waterhouse

Artwork Archivist Steve Robinson

Index Sue Lightfoot

The author wishes to thank the editorial and
design teams for their help with this book.

KINGFISHER

Kingfisher Publications Plc
New Penderel House
283–288 High Holborn
London WC1V 7HZ
www.kingfisherpub.com

First published by Kingfisher Publications Plc 1999

2 4 6 8 10 9 7 5 3 1 (HB)

ITR/0499/TWP/FR/AMA150

2 4 6 8 10 9 7 5 3 1 (PB)

1TR/0301/TEP/RNB/130ARM

Copyright © Kingfisher Publications Plc 1999
First published in paperback in 2001

A CIP catalogue record for this book is available from the British Library.

ISBN 0 7534 0312 9 (HB)
ISBN 0 7534 0568 7 (PB)

Printed in Singapore

Your book

Your *First Encyclopedia of the Human Body* is the perfect way of finding out all about the human body. Packed with exciting information, amazing facts and colourful pictures, it can be used for school projects or just for fun.

△ The information about each picture is printed next to it. The arrows show you which information goes with which picture.

this muscle straightens the fingers

a band of fibres holds the tendons in place

▷ Labels on some pictures give extra information. Follow the lines to find out what the different parts do.

tendon from the muscle that straightens the fingers

Kidney sieve

Mix together some salt and sugar and shake it in a sieve over a bowl. The salt passes through the sieve while the sugar stays in it. Your kidneys 'sieve' blood so that you lose waste but keep nutrients.

△ Instructions and photographs in the coloured boxes show you how to do the activities.

Find Out More

If you want to find out more about any topic, look at this box. It will tell you which pages to look at.

Contents

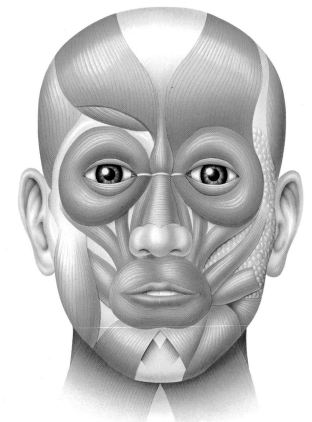

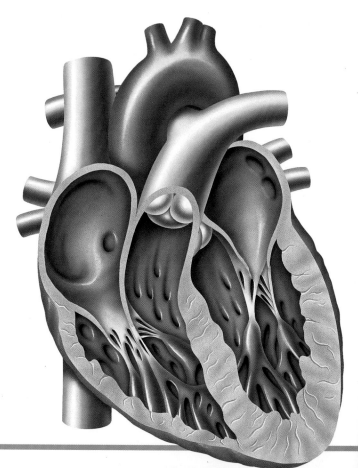

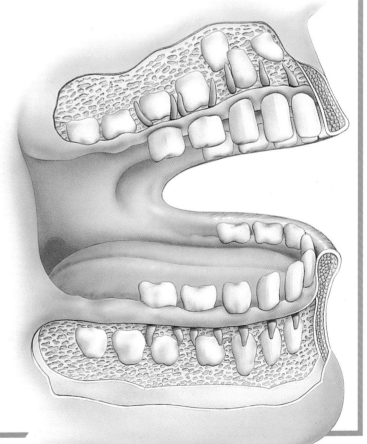

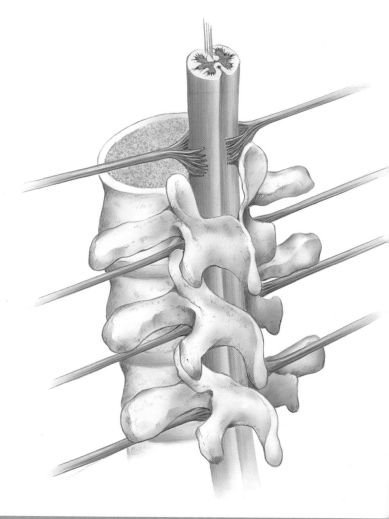

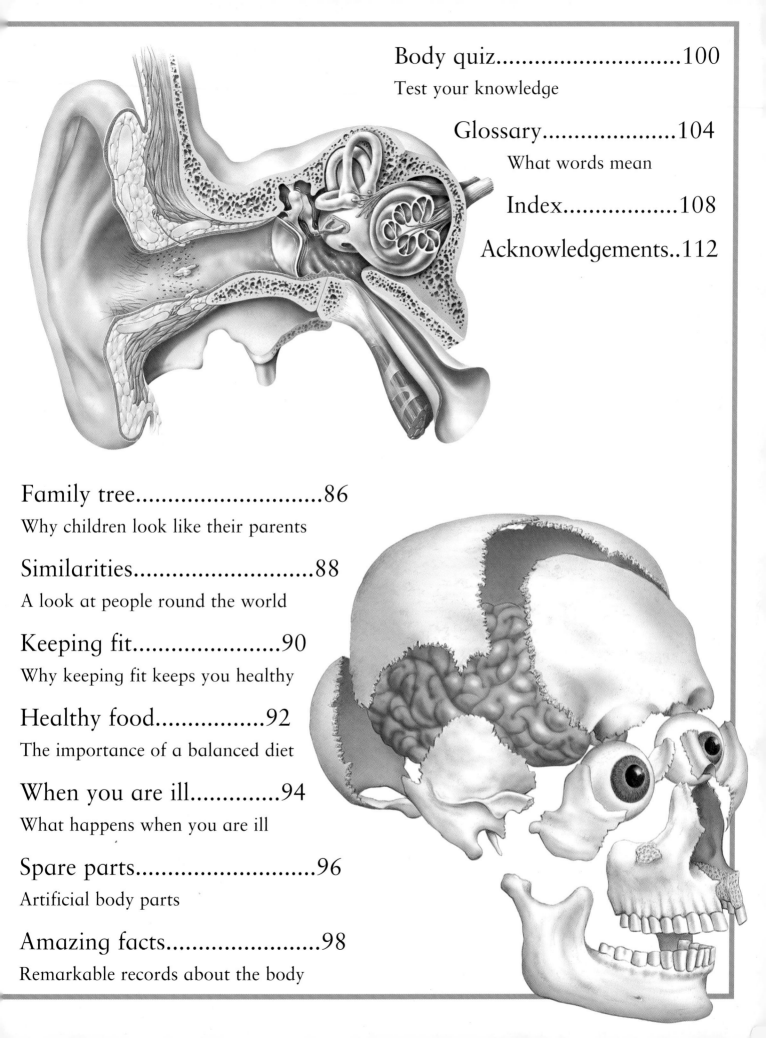

Our bodies

Sit quietly for a moment. Listen to yourself breathing. Put your hand in the centre of your chest and feel your heart beating. Think about what you would most like to do in the world. Now consider the fact that these body activities – breathing, the beating of your heart and the ability to think – are at the same time being experienced by another six billion people.

△ Variety is the spice of life! Look at this group of children and you can see different heights, different skin colours, different faces and different hair. However, although we all look very different from each other, we can all share in the fact that we belong to the human family.

△ Humans divide equally into two main groups – females and males. The differences between them become more obvious when they are grown up. Women have more rounded bodies with broader hips, while men usually have more muscular bodies with broader shoulders.

▷ Two-thirds of your body is made up of water. You need to drink to replace the water that you lose when you sweat or go to the toilet.

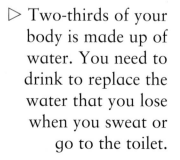

△ Everyone needs to eat. Food provides you with the energy your body needs to keep it running normally. It also gives you building material to allow you to grow.

your face can produce many different expressions to show how you feel

your heart and lungs are protected inside your chest

your abdomen contains the parts of the body that digest food for energy

your arms bend at the shoulder and elbow to move in all directions

▷ Your head contains your brain – the body's control centre. Your trunk (the central part of the body) is divided into the chest and abdomen, which contain many of your most vital organs. Attached to your trunk are your arms, which let you pick up and hold objects, and your legs, which support your body and allow you to walk.

your legs support your body and allow you to walk, run and jump

your feet allow you to stand without toppling over

Find Out More

Similarities 88–89

Keeping fit 90–91

Cells

Your body is made up of millions and millions of microscopic cells. Each cell is a tiny, living unit with a complex inner structure. There are many different types of cells in the body, each with its own shape, size and job to do. Cells of the same type are grouped together as tissue.

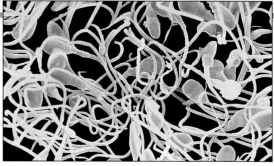

△ Every sperm cell has a head and a tail. Sperm swim along by lashing their tails from side to side.

▷ A muscle cell is sometimes called a muscle fibre. To make your body move, the long, stripy muscle fibres contract (get shorter) and pull on your bones.

◁ Your liver is packed with cube-shaped cells. Blood flows along the spaces between them. As it does so, liver cells busily clean the blood and make sure it contains the correct ingredients.

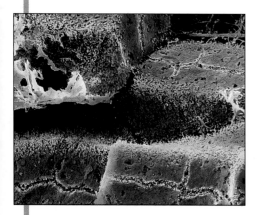

membrane surrounds the cell

▷ Looking like doughnut-shaped cushions, red blood cells carry life-giving oxygen to where it is needed. The blood cells tumble over each other as blood surges along an artery (a tube that carries blood around the body).

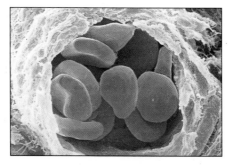

jelly-like substance contains organelles

▽ Cells may appear different from the outside, but inside they look much like this. Each cell has a nucleus (centre) that controls what it does. It also has many different organelles ('tiny organs') that keep the cell working properly.

▷ This liver cell is one of many different kinds of cell inside the body.

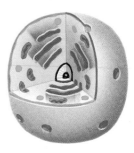

these channels move substances around the cell

mitochondria are organelles that supply energy

▷ Liver cells of the same type are grouped together to form tissue.

ribosomes are organelles that make cell-building proteins

▷ Together, different tissues form an organ, in this case the liver.

nucleus (centre) of the cell

▷ The liver and other organs form the digestive system.

▷ Inside your brain there are billions of nerve cells. Each has branches that connect it to other nerve cells. Messages flash along these branches so that you can think and feel.

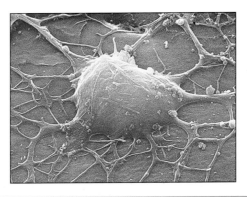

Find Out More

Hormones
54–55

Egg and sperm
78–79

Outer covering

Your skin covers your body like a living overcoat. Although it is only 2 mm thick, skin forms a barrier between you and the outside world. It stops germs getting inside your body, protects you from damage and the harmful rays in sunlight, and makes sure you do not dry out.

hair

◁ A closer look at the skin reveals a criss-cross pattern of lines. The hairs grow from holes called follicles.

epidermis {

▷ Under the microscope, the surface of the skin looks scaly and flaky. Every year 4 kg of flakes are worn away from your skin.

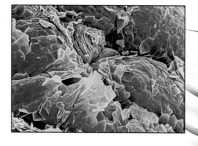

Looking at skin

To see what your skin really looks like, use a magnifying glass. Hold it above your arm and then move it slowly until the skin's surface comes into focus. What can you see? Is your skin smooth, or are there lines or wrinkles? Can you see any skin flakes? Now look at the skin on your fingertips. Can you see any patterns? Are there any hairs?

dermis

sweat gland

sweat pore

hair
follicle

blood vessels

layer of fat

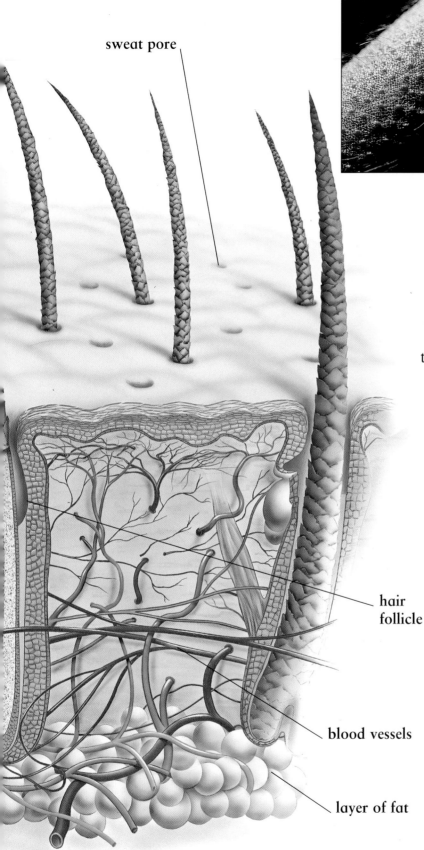

◁ If you get cold or scared, goosebumps like these appear on your skin. This happens because tiny muscles in the skin tug the hair follicles, making the hairs stand upright, and the skin go bumpy!

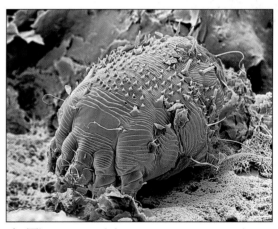

▷ This microscopic picture shows droplets of sweat on the skin of someone who is hot from doing exercise. As the sweat evaporates, it takes heat from the body and helps to cool it down.

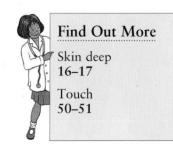

△ Tiny parasitic creatures sometimes live on human skin. Skin mites feed on skin flakes. Itch mites, like the one pictured here, burrow into the skin to lay eggs.

Find Out More

Skin deep
16–17

Touch
50–51

△ Skin has two layers – the epidermis and the dermis. The epidermis forms a protective covering. Its cells are constantly worn away and replaced. The dermis contains sweat glands and blood vessels. A layer of fat under the dermis helps to keep you warm.

Skin deep

The colour of your skin is produced by the thin, outer epidermis. It contains melanin, a brown pigment (colouring) which helps protect the dermis from the harmful effects of sunlight. Exposed to sunlight, your skin naturally makes extra melanin to darken your skin and provide extra protection.

◁ An umbrella stops your clothes getting wet when it rains. Your epidermis forms a waterproof layer that stops water seeping into your body.

◁ Normally the temperature inside your body stays the same. A layer of fat under the skin helps to keep it warm. Unless the weather is very hot, you also need to wear clothes to keep the heat in.

▷ Sunlight can burn your skin or, in some cases, cause a serious disease called skin cancer. Suntan creams and sunblocks rubbed onto the skin, as well as hats and loose clothes, all help stop sunlight from damaging your skin.

▽ These babies show the wide variety of skin colours found in human beings. Human skin colours range through thousands of shades from pale pink to very dark brown. Skin colour depends on how much melanin is made by the epidermis. The more melanin present, the darker a person's skin. Pale skin is given a pinkish colour by the blood flowing just below its surface.

Making skin lighter
Your skin naturally gets darker in sunlight. But what happens if you cover it up? Take a sticking plaster and wrap it round one finger. Leave it in place for a few days and then remove it. You will find that the skin covered by the plaster has got lighter in colour. The plaster stops sunlight from reaching the skin, so it makes less melanin.

△ This girl has freckles on her face. These are tiny patches of skin that contain more than the usual amount of melanin. Freckles are more easily seen on people with lighter skin.

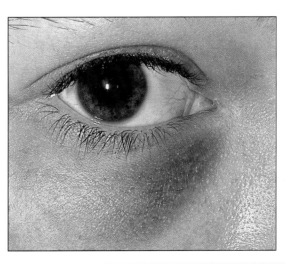

▷ If your skin is hit or knocked, some of the tiny blood vessels in it may break and leak. You can see this leakage of blood as a bruise. Bruises are normally blue or black at first, but then turn yellow. A bruise near the eye is usually called a 'black eye'.

Find Out More
Outer covering
14–15
Hands
30–31

All about hair

Although millions of hairs cover your body, they are mostly too short and fine to keep you warm. Only the long hairs on your head keep in heat. Hairs grow from pits in the skin called follicles. Head hair grows about two millimetres a week for a few years, then growth stops. The hair falls out and is replaced by a new one.

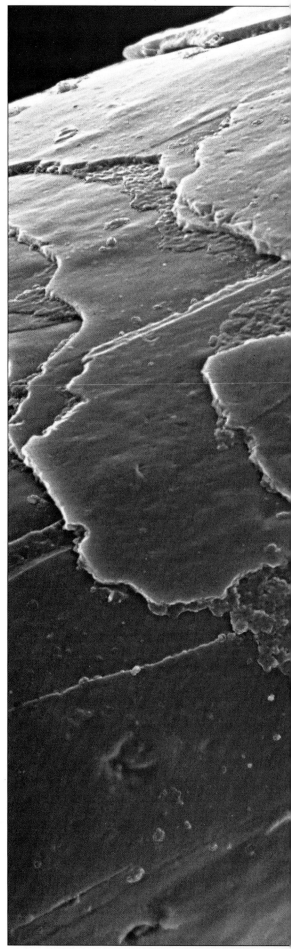

◁ Some men are bald because their head hairs grow for only a short time. The hairs do not grow long enough to stick out from the follicles before falling out.

▷ Long, thick hair grows on men's faces. Many men shave daily to remove this hair. Others let it grow into a moustache and beard.

Hairy sensors

Carefully run your fingers over the hairs on your arms without touching the surface of your skin. You should feel the sensation of very light touch even though your finger does not make contact with your skin. As you touch the hairs you move the touch sensors at their base. The sensors send signals to the brain so that you can feel even the gentlest touch.

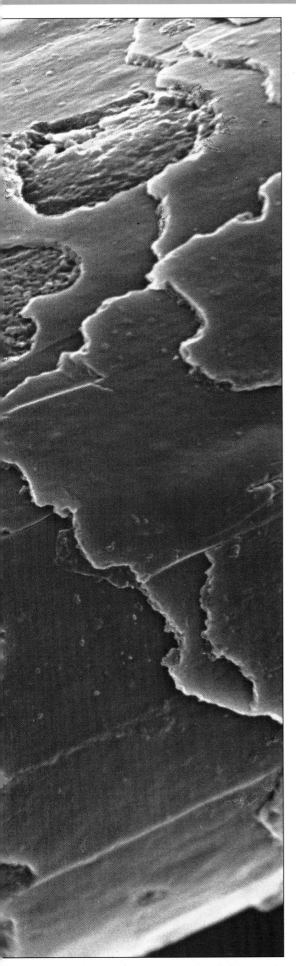

△ Hair colour ranges from blonde to black according to the amount of melanin, the brown pigment that also colours skin. Hair can be straight, wavy or curly depending on the shape of the follicles from which the hair grows.

▷ Straight hairs grow from hair follicles that are rounded in shape.

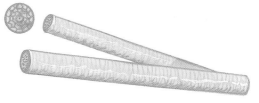

▷ Wavy hairs grow from hair follicles that are oval in shape.

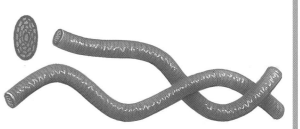

▷ Curly hairs grow from hair follicles that are flattened in shape.

◁ This is a highly magnified view of a hair. The outside of the hair is covered by plates that overlap like fish scales. They stop hairs from sticking together. Hair cells are dead. This is why it does not hurt when you have your hair cut.

Find Out More

Our bodies
10–11

Outer covering
14–15

Bony frame

Your body is supported by a bony frame called the skeleton. This is made of 206 bones that link together to form a strong but flexible framework. The skeleton protects important organs, such as the brain and heart, and anchors the muscles that allow you to move. Before birth, the skeleton is made of a bendy material called cartilage.

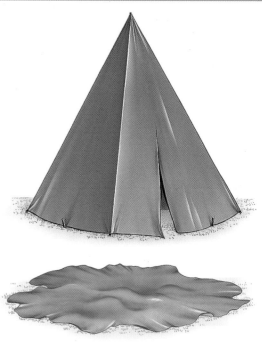

△ Tent poles support a tent and give it shape. Without them, the tent collapses and is shapeless. Your skeleton does exactly the same job for your body. Without your bones, your body would immediately collapse into a floppy mess.

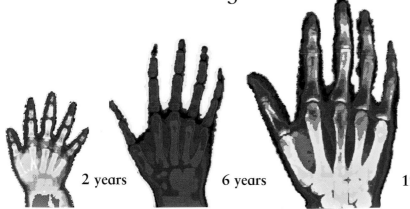

2 years   6 years   19 years

△ As you grow, most cartilage is replaced by harder bone. In these X-rays, bone shows up but cartilage does not. In a two-year-old's hand, there are big gaps between bones where cartilage is present. By six years old, bone is replacing cartilage. In an adult hand, the bones are fully formed and there is little cartilage.

Feel your cartilage

To find out what cartilage feels like, hold your ear and gently bend and twist it. Your ear is supported by cartilage. Although it holds your ear in position, it is easy to move, and not hard like bone. Feel the end of your nose too. This is also supported by cartilage.

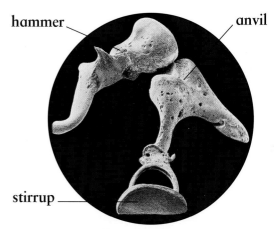

hammer   anvil

stirrup

△ Your smallest bones are the three tiny ossicles in your ear. They are also called the hammer, anvil and stirrup because of their shapes. They help carry sounds into your ear, so you can hear. The tiniest one, the stirrup, is just 3 mm long.

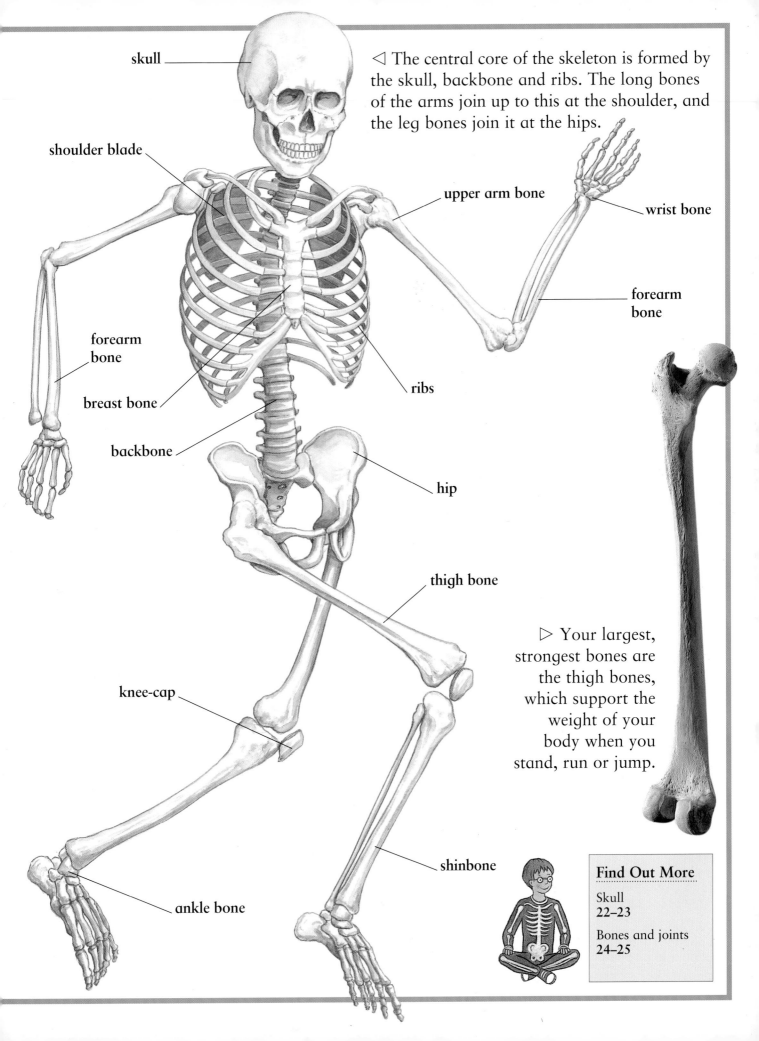

skull

shoulder blade

◁ The central core of the skeleton is formed by the skull, backbone and ribs. The long bones of the arms join up to this at the shoulder, and the leg bones join it at the hips.

upper arm bone

wrist bone

forearm bone

forearm bone

breast bone

ribs

backbone

hip

thigh bone

▷ Your largest, strongest bones are the thigh bones, which support the weight of your body when you stand, run or jump.

knee-cap

shinbone

ankle bone

Find Out More

Skull
22–23

Bones and joints
24–25

Skull

Your bony skull gives shape to your head and face. It surrounds the soft, delicate brain and prevents it from being crushed or damaged. Openings in the skull form entrances to the ears, nose and mouth. The eye sockets act like protective pockets, allowing the eyes to swivel. Rows of strong teeth are firmly anchored in the jaw bones, ready to bite and chew food.

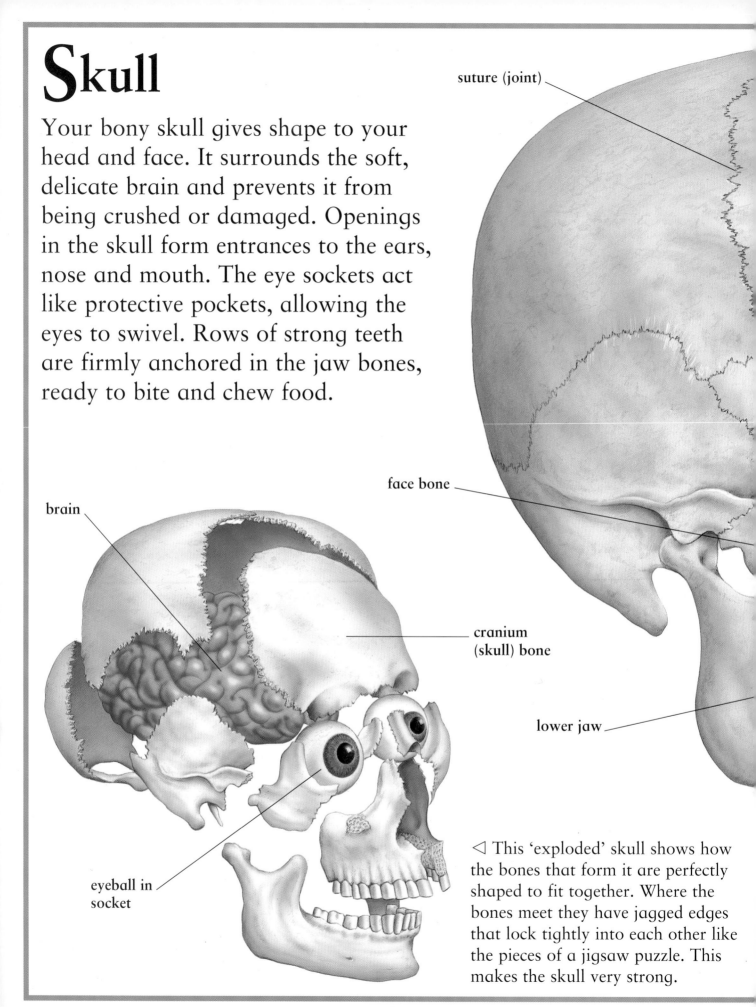

suture (joint)

face bone

cranium (skull) bone

lower jaw

brain

eyeball in socket

◁ This 'exploded' skull shows how the bones that form it are perfectly shaped to fit together. Where the bones meet they have jagged edges that lock tightly into each other like the pieces of a jigsaw puzzle. This makes the skull very strong.

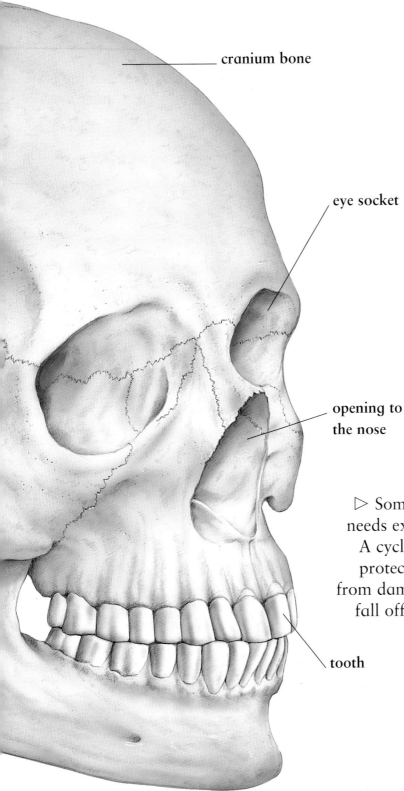

cranium bone

eye socket

opening to
the nose

tooth

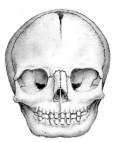

Face and skull aged 6

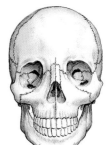

Face and skull aged 16

△ During childhood, our faces change in shape and appearance. This happens because the bones of the face grow rapidly as we get older.

▷ Sometimes the head needs extra protection. A cycle helmet will protect your skull from damage if you fall off your bike.

△ The skull is made up of 22 bones. Eight form the cranium, the bony box which surrounds the brain. The other 14 bones make up the face. Nearly all the bones are firmly locked together by unmoving joints called sutures. Only the lower jaw is able to move freely, allowing you to eat and speak.

Find Out More

Bones and joints
24–25

Control centre
34–35

Bones and joints

Bones are living organs with their own cells and blood supply. They are formed from materials that make them both hard and strong. In the skeleton, bones meet at joints. Most joints are moveable, and this allows the skeleton to change position. Different joints allow different kinds of movement.

▽ Bones have an outer layer of compact bone that is very hard. It surrounds a layer of lighter spongy bone. The hollow centre of the bone is filled with jelly-like bone marrow. This structure makes living bones five times stronger than steel.

a membrane protects the bone

spongy bone

compact bone

◁ Hinge joints work like a door hinge. They allow bones to move up and down but not from side to side. You can see a hinge joint in action when you bend or straighten your knee.

Hinge joint

▷ Ball and socket joints allow movement in many directions. The rounded end of one bone fits inside the cup-shaped socket of another bone. In the shoulder, the end of the arm bone fits into a socket formed by the shoulder bones.

Ball and socket joint

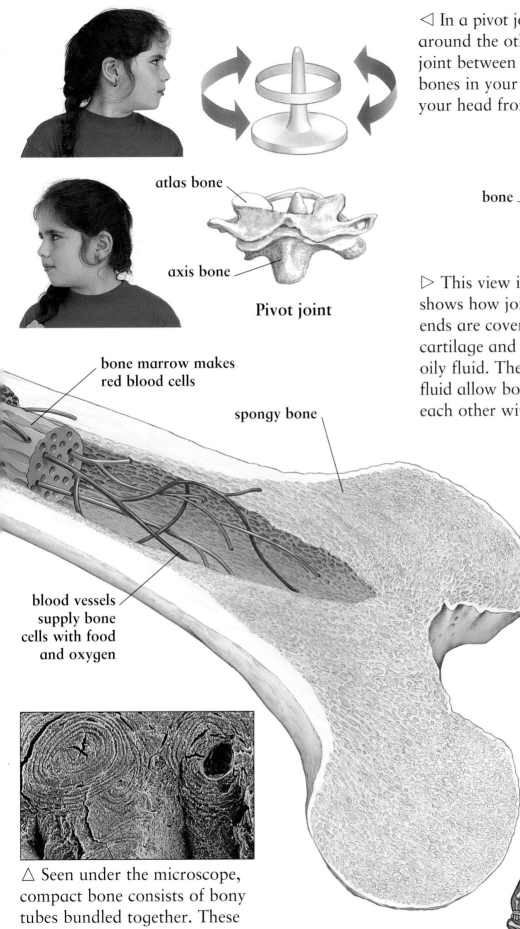

◁ In a pivot joint, one bone swivels around the other one. The pivot joint between the atlas and axis bones in your neck lets you turn your head from side to side.

atlas bone

axis bone

Pivot joint

cartilage

bone

▷ This view inside the knee shows how joints work. Bone ends are covered with shiny cartilage and separated by oily fluid. The cartilage and fluid allow bones to slide over each other without rubbing.

fluid

bone marrow makes red blood cells

spongy bone

blood vessels supply bone cells with food and oxygen

△ Spongy bone is a honeycomb of spaces and bony struts. The spaces are filled with bone marrow.

△ Seen under the microscope, compact bone consists of bony tubes bundled together. These make the bone very strong.

Find Out More

Bony frame
20–21

Muscle power
26–27

Muscle power

Every movement that you make uses muscles. Without them, you could not run, walk, smile or speak. Muscles can contract when told to do so by the brain. Each muscle is attached to two or more bones by tough cords called tendons. When the muscle contracts, it pulls on the bones and makes the body move.

▷ Every time you move, your brain has to control many muscles at once. Some activities, like running, need hundreds of muscles to be working together at the same time. To move with the skill and grace of a dancer you need strong muscles and plenty of practice.

▷ The muscles that move the body lie just under the skin. As well as producing movement, they give the body its shape. Here, you can see some of a dancer's main muscles and what they do. You have the same muscles in your body.

running

going head over heels

Flex your muscles

Muscles often work together in pairs. Each muscle can only pull – it cannot push. One muscle, the biceps, bends your arm, and another, the triceps, straightens it. See if you can feel them changing shape as you move your arm.

biceps contracts and pulls arm up

Arm bent

Arm straight

triceps contracts and pulls arm down

biceps relaxes

muscle attached to bone by tendon

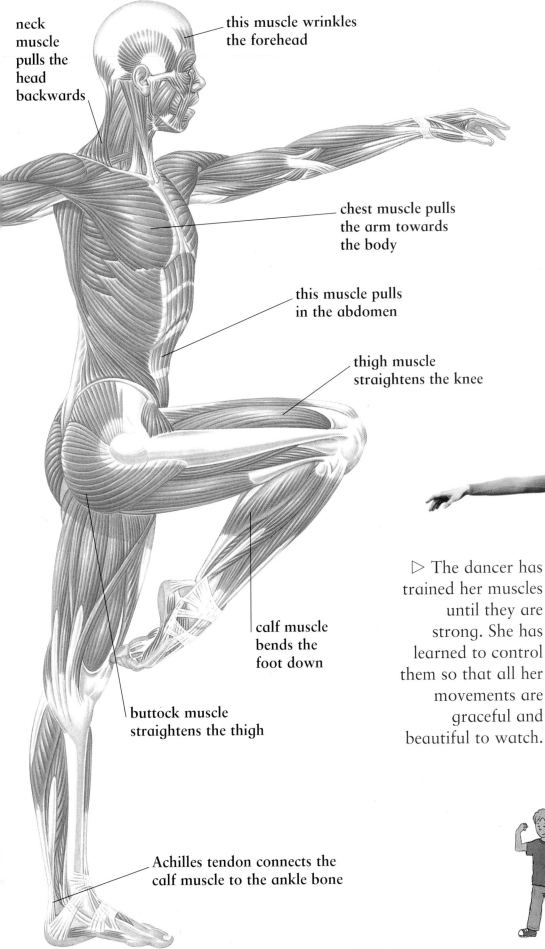

neck muscle pulls the head backwards

this muscle wrinkles the forehead

chest muscle pulls the arm towards the body

this muscle pulls in the abdomen

thigh muscle straightens the knee

calf muscle bends the foot down

buttock muscle straightens the thigh

Achilles tendon connects the calf muscle to the ankle bone

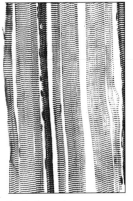

△ Muscles are made of long cells called fibres, which look stripy under a microscope. These contract when the brain tells them to.

▷ The dancer has trained her muscles until they are strong. She has learned to control them so that all her movements are graceful and beautiful to watch.

Find Out More

Muscles at work
28–29

Control centre
34–35

Muscles at work

There are over 640 skeletal muscles in your body. They produce a wide range of movements depending on their size and strength, and the bones and joints with which they work. Muscles in the face and neck make facial expressions. Other muscles support your body when you are awake. As muscles work, they release heat. This helps keep your body warm.

this muscle pulls down the eyebrow

this muscle pulls on the corner of the mouth

this muscle closes the mouth

this muscle purses the lips

△ When you frown, muscles pull your eyebrows down and towards each other.

△ If you feel sad, muscles in your chin pull the corners of your mouth downwards.

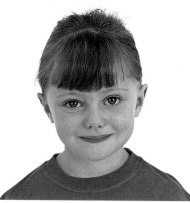

△ To smile, muscles in your cheeks pull the corners of your mouth upwards.

△ When you look surprised, muscles raise your eyebrows and open your eyes wide.

this muscle
wrinkles the
forehead and
raises the
eyebrow

Tiring muscles

Make a fist and then open it. Now repeat this as quickly and as often as possible. You will soon have to stop as your muscles get tired. This is because skeletal muscle can work very hard, but it tires easily and needs to rest. Compare this with your amazing heart muscles. They make the heart beat for a lifetime and never stop or get tired.

this muscle
closes the
eyelids

this muscle
raises the
upper lip

these muscles
pull the mouth
into a smile

this muscle pulls
down the lower lip

this muscle pulls
down the corners
of the mouth

△ The muscles of this sleeping boy have relaxed and provide less support for his body. The girl is awake and her muscles keep her upright.

△ After exercise, this man's muscles are hot and show up white in a heat picture. When cool, they are darker.

△ These are some of the muscles that pull on the skin of your face to produce expressions such as smiling or frowning. These expressions communicate your feelings to other people.

Find Out More

Communication
52–53

Inside the heart
56–57

Hands

Each of your hands contains 27 bones, making them the most flexible part of your body. Unlike most other animals, humans walk upright so that their hands are free to act as tools. Over 30 muscles in the forearm and hands move your wrists, palms, thumbs and fingers. This allows you to perform all kinds of tasks.

▽ Most of the muscles that move your fingers are found not in the hand, but in the arm. They are attached to the hand and finger bones by very long tendons. You can see your own tendons move by looking at the back of your hand and bending your fingers.

this muscle straightens the fingers

this muscle straightens the wrist

a band of fibres holds the tendons in place

△ Some people – and you may be one of them – have difficulty using their hands. This does not stop them from drawing or writing, however. This woman is using a special head attachment to help her draw.

Tied fingers

Write your name on a piece of paper. Now take a rubber band and wrap it round your fingers so that they cannot move. Try to write your name again. It is very difficult. Your fingers must be free to form the special grip that you use to write.

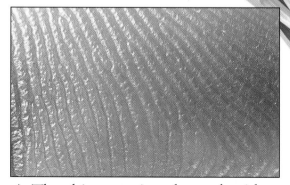

△ The skin covering the undersides of your fingers and palms is not smooth. It is covered by tiny ridges that help you to grip objects.

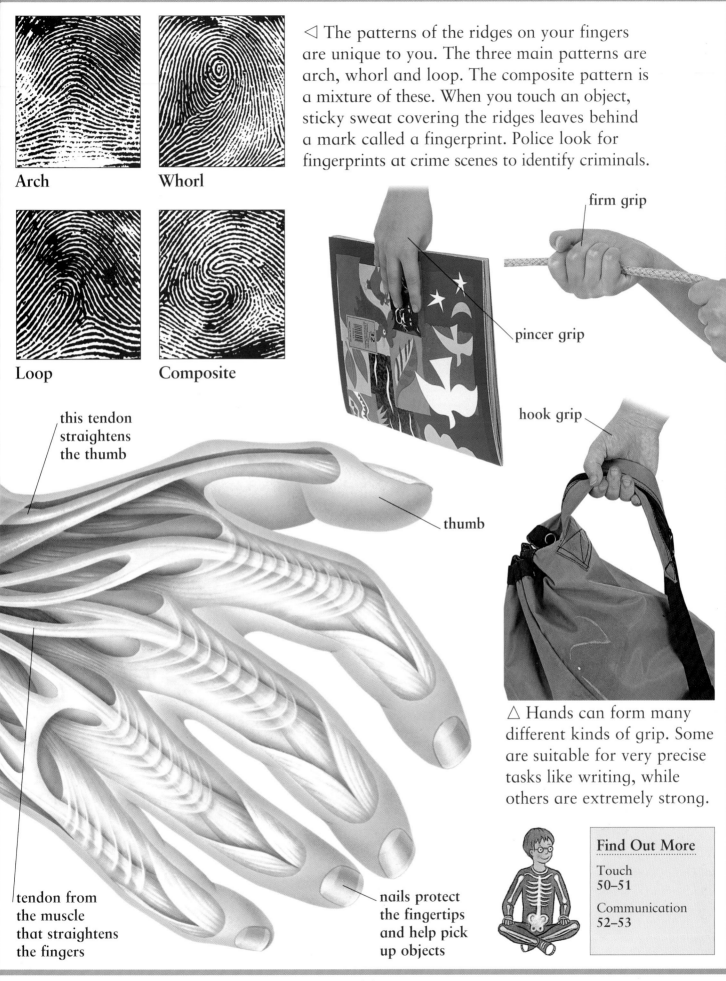

Arch

Whorl

Loop

Composite

◁ The patterns of the ridges on your fingers are unique to you. The three main patterns are arch, whorl and loop. The composite pattern is a mixture of these. When you touch an object, sticky sweat covering the ridges leaves behind a mark called a fingerprint. Police look for fingerprints at crime scenes to identify criminals.

firm grip

pincer grip

hook grip

thumb

this tendon straightens the thumb

tendon from the muscle that straightens the fingers

nails protect the fingertips and help pick up objects

△ Hands can form many different kinds of grip. Some are suitable for very precise tasks like writing, while others are extremely strong.

Find Out More

Touch 50–51

Communication 52–53

Control centre

Your body's control centre is the brain. It gives you the ability to think, feel, move, remember, and be happy or sad. It also controls all the other parts of the body. The thinking, feeling part of the brain is called the cerebrum. Its left half controls the right side of your body, and its right half controls the left.

◁ The brain's movement area sends messages to your muscles, telling them to contract so that your body moves.

movement area

sensory area

▷ Millions of touch sensors in your skin send messages to your brain's sensory area. They help you feel whether things are hard or soft.

vision area

◁ Your eyes send a non-stop stream of messages to the vision area at the back of the brain. This turns the messages into pictures that you can see.

Use your brain

Look at this picture of the brain – it is the same as the bigger one in the middle of the page – and try to answer this quiz. Which part of the brain are you using when you a) read these words, b) turn a page, c) touch the picture, d) work out the answers to these questions?

Answers: a) 1; b) 3; c) 2; d) 6

△ Hearing areas receive nerve messages from your ears and turn them into sounds you can hear.

◁ This baby has never been swimming before, but when he is put into water he automatically moves his arms and legs in a swimming motion. Another reflex action stops him breathing in while his head is under water.

5 The nerve message arrives in the brain and the girl feels pain.

3 A motor neuron carries a message to the arm muscle.

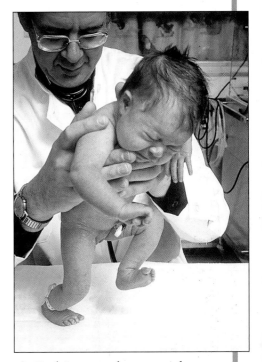

4 The arm muscle jerks the finger away.

△ Babies are born with a set of simple, built-in reflexes. One of these is the walking reflex. When the doctor holds the baby with her feet touching the ground, she makes walking movements. These reflexes disappear after a few months.

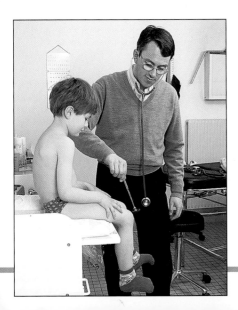

◁ Doctors use reflexes to test whether the nervous system is working well. Here a doctor gently taps the boy's knee with a hammer. When he does this, the boy's lower leg should move. This shows that nerve messages are passing normally between the knee, the spinal cord and the muscles in the leg.

Find Out More

Nervous network 32–33

All about babies 82–83

Learning

From birth to late teens, humans learn the skills they need in life. Learning depends on memory, the ability the brain has to store and recall lots of information. Movement skills, such as walking, are learned by trial and error. Languages and facts and figures are learned by listening and reading.

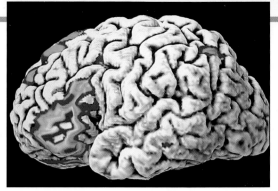

△ To speak you need to learn words. This picture shows the area in the brain that is active when you speak.

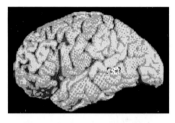
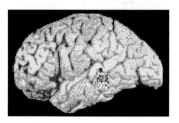

◁ Seeing and listening play an important part in learning. These scans show the brain at work taking in new information. In the top scan, the person is seeing words in a book. In the bottom scan, she is hearing words spoken.

△ Playing chess is a skilful activity. First, you have to learn the moves that each chess piece can make. As you get more experienced, you start to learn how to combine these moves on the board. Only then are you able plan several moves in advance in order to defeat your opponent.

△ In a language laboratory, a class listens to their teacher as they learn a foreign language. To learn a new language, you have to listen to it or read it, and then store the words away in your memory. The more you practise, the easier it becomes to remember the words.

◁ By hanging on to a chair, this baby is able to pull herself upright. Once she gets used to standing up, she will take her first steps. She will slowly learn to walk by trial and error. If she moves and does not fall over, this experience will be stored in her memory.

△ This girl uses a trolley to give her extra support as she walks. As she learns to walk in a more controlled way, her movements become less jerky. Every time she tries it, she improves a little.

△ At the age of one, this girl can stand up and take a few steps without any support. But she still loses her balance from time to time and falls over.

◁ Cycling is another skill that has to be learned. This child can pedal with her feet to move the bicycle forward, and she can steer with her hands. She is not yet able to balance without stabilizers for support.

Find Out More

Control centre
34–35

Growing up
84–85

Sleep

Sleep is essential for health. It allows your body to rest, and your brain to sort the information it received that day. People deprived of sleep soon become ill. Every night, you have periods of deep sleep, when your brain is not very active. During lighter sleep, when your brain is active, your eyes move under your eyelids and you dream.

◁ In the evening, your brain activity changes as it gets ready for sleep. You want to lie down because you are too tired to stand or sit, and your eyelids feel heavy and start to close. Now you are ready for bed.

△ The number of hours you need to sleep each night gets fewer as you get older. Babies sleep for 16 hours each day, but a five-year-old child needs only about 12 hours' sleep. Adults need about eight hours' sleep.

Keep a dream diary

When you wake each morning, write down the details of any dreams you can remember. You will probably find that your dreams mix up many events, facts and people. This is because dreams happen while the brain is sorting out all the messages it received during the day and comparing them with information already stored in the memory.

△ You usually wake in a different position to the one you went to sleep in. This is because you move during deep sleep. During lighter sleep, your muscles are paralysed to stop you acting out your dreams!

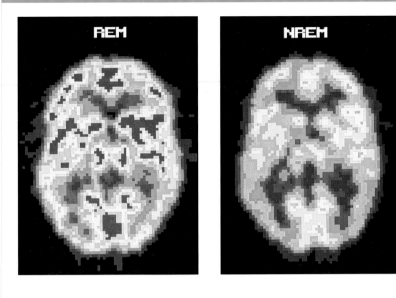
REM   NREM

◁ These pictures are produced by a machine called a PET scanner. This scans a person's brain to see which parts of it are active. Active areas are red and inactive areas are blue. The left scan shows a person in light, dreaming sleep. The right scan shows a person in deep sleep. You can see that the brain is more active in light sleep than deep sleep.

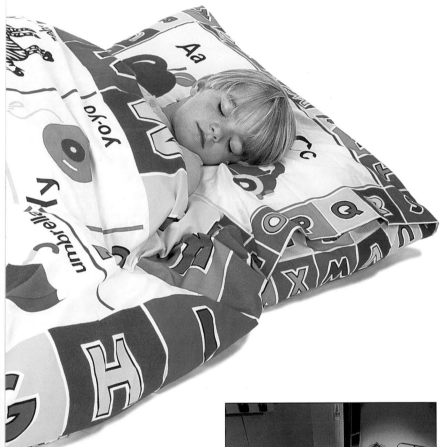

△ This patient is about to have an operation in hospital. A doctor is giving her gas to keep her unconscious during the operation. She will feel no pain and cannot wake up as she could do if she was asleep.

▷ Your brain produces electrical signals called brain-waves. These alter as you go from deep to light sleep. Here, the pattern of a sleeper's brain-waves are being recorded by a machine.

Find Out More

Control centre
34–35

Learning
38–39

Eye facts

Your eyes are carefully protected. The exposed parts of the eye, not protected by the bony eye sockets, are washed with tears whenever your eyelids blink. Eyelids cover the eyes to protect them from damage, and eyelashes keep out dust. Eyes may not work properly for a number of reasons. Fortunately, there are several ways in which these vision problems can be overcome.

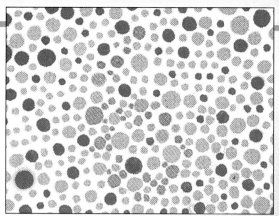

△ Some people, usually males, are said to be colour blind because they cannot tell certain colours apart. They lack one of the three types of cones (sensors) that detect red, green or blue light. If you can see the number six in this pattern of dots you are not colour blind.

▷ Blind people cannot use their eyes to read. The Braille reading system allows them to read using touch. Instead of written words, Braille uses patterns of raised dots, in groups of up to six, on paper or card. Sensitive fingertips feel the dot patterns and 'read' the words.

◁ Short-sighted people cannot see distant objects clearly. Long-sighted people cannot see nearby objects clearly. In both cases light is not focused properly inside the eye. Short-sighted and long-sighted people can wear glasses or contact lenses to correct their vision.

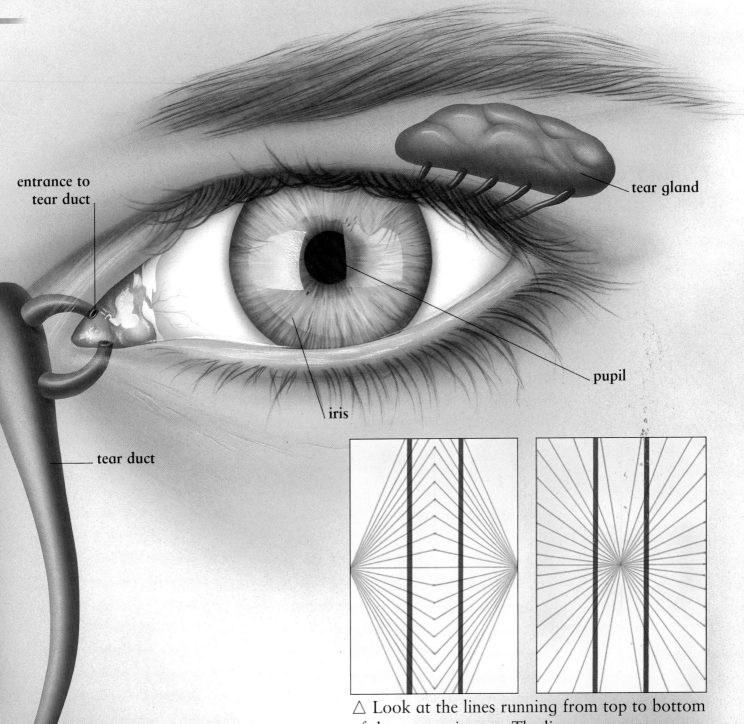

entrance to
tear duct

tear gland

pupil

iris

tear duct

opening
inside nose

△ Look at the lines running from top to bottom of these two pictures. The lines appear to curve inwards (left) and outwards (right). In fact, both sets of lines are straight. Your brain was tricked by the patterns into 'seeing' the curves. Tricks like these are called optical illusions.

△ The front of your eye is kept clean and moist by tears. Tears are produced by tear glands that empty onto the surface of your eye. Every time you blink, tears wash away dirt and dust and kill germs on your eye. The liquid then drains into tear ducts that connect with your nose.

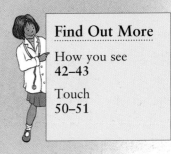

Find Out More

How you see
42–43

Touch
50–51

How you hear

From the music of a violin to the roar of a motorbike, your ears allow you to hear thousands of different sounds. Most of each ear is hidden inside the skull. Sounds travel through the ear until they reach the snail-shaped cochlea. Sensors in the cochlea send nerve messages to the brain so you can 'hear' the sound.

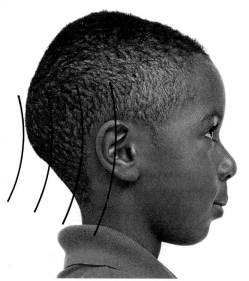

△ Sounds travel in waves through the air until they reach your ears.

the pinna funnels sound into the ear

ear canal

Balancing act
The semicircular canals in your ears detect the movement and position of your head. This information allows your brain to help you balance. Your brain also receives information from your eyes and feet. Stand on a cushion, put your arms out, raise one leg and close your eyes. Is it easy to balance?

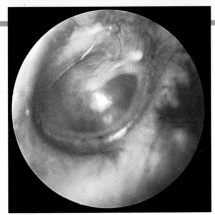

△ Using an instrument called an otoscope a doctor can examine the ear canal and ear drum inside the ear.

◁ Sound waves send ripples through the liquid in the cochlea. These ripples bend filaments (yellow 'v' shapes) which are linked to special cells that send sound messages to the brain.

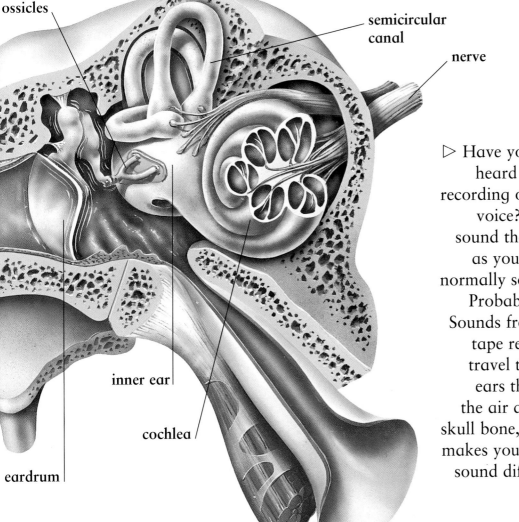

ossicles

semicircular canal

nerve

inner ear

cochlea

eardrum

▷ Have you ever heard a tape recording of your voice? Did it sound the same as your voice normally sounds? Probably not. Sounds from the tape recorder travel to your ears through the air and the skull bone, which makes your voice sound different.

△ Sound waves hit the eardrum and make it vibrate. These vibrations pass along three tiny bones called the ossicles which create ripples in the fluid filling the inner ear. When these ripples reach the cochlea, it sends messages to the brain.

Find Out More

Touch
50–51

Communication
52–53

Taste and smell

Your senses of taste and smell detect chemicals in food and air. Chemicals in food are detected by sensors called taste buds in your tongue. Chemicals in the air are detected by smell sensors in your nose. The sensors send messages to the brain so that you 'taste' or 'smell'. You can detect many smells, but only four tastes.

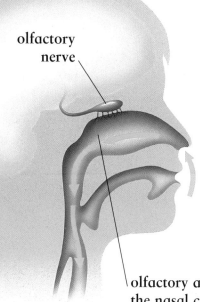

olfactory nerve

olfactory area in the nasal cavity

◁ The nasal cavity carries air to your throat when you breathe in. At the top of the nasal cavity is the olfactory (smelling) area where sensors pick up smells in the air. The sensors send messages to the brain along the olfactory nerve.

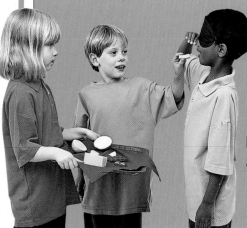

What's that food?

Ask an adult to cut different foods, such as apple and onion, into bite-size chunks. Blindfold a friend and ask them to hold their nose. Put pieces of food in your friend's mouth. Can they identify them by taste alone?

◁ Your sense of smell warns you about bad odours!

▷ Inside each taste bud is a bundle of sensors that resemble the segments of an orange. When chemicals from food enter the taste bud through an opening called the taste pore, the sensors send messages to the brain.

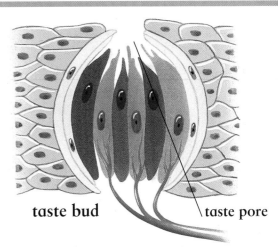

taste bud **taste pore**

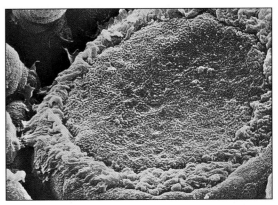

△ This is one of the large papillae (bumps) found at the back of your tongue. Taste buds are located in the sides of these papillae.

bitter taste area

sour taste area

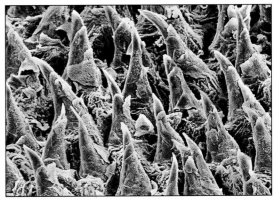

△ Pointed papillae are found all over your tongue. They make the tongue rough and help it grip food.

salt taste area

sweet taste area

◁ Four distinct tastes are detected by taste buds – sweet, salt, sour and bitter. Taste buds at the front of the tongue detect sweet, those at the side detect salt and sour, and those at the back detect bitter tastes.

Find Out More

Why you eat
70–71

Digesting food
74–75

Touch

Millions of sensors in your skin send a non-stop stream of messages to your brain so that you can touch and feel your surroundings. Some sensors detect light touch, some sense vibration or pressure, while others sense heat, cold or pain. Working together, different sensors give your brain a 'touch picture'.

▽ This view inside the skin shows the different sensors found there. Some lie deep in the dermis, while others reach up into the epidermis. Nerve fibres carry messages from the sensors to the brain.

◁ Some parts of your skin have many more touch sensors than others, making them much more sensitive. This picture of a boy looks odd because the size of his body parts are drawn according to how sensitive they are.

light touch and pressure sensors

heavy pressure sensors

sensors around hair

What's that object?

Put some different objects – such as a tennis ball, orange and tomato – onto a tray. Blindfold a friend and ask them to tell you what each object is by feeling it. Repeat this with your friend wearing gloves. How many can they identify now?

◁ If you put an ice cube in your hand, the sudden temperature drop makes cold sensors send messages to your brain.

◁ This boy is running his fingertips over a piece of sandpaper. As the skin of his fingers is pulled and prodded by the surface of the sandpaper, sensors send messages to his brain. This tells him that sandpaper is rough and covered by thousands of tiny, hard particles.

light pressure sensor

epidermis

dermis

sensor for heat, cold and pain

△ Sensors for light touch allow you to feel the softness of an animal's fur. At the same time, heat sensors in the skin tell you that the animal is warm as well as soft.

◁ Sensors in the fingers of the boy's right hand sense the light touch needed to hold a delicate flower stem. Sensors in the palm of the left hand sense the pressure produced by the vase filled with water.

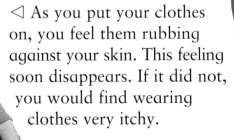

◁ As you put your clothes on, you feel them rubbing against your skin. This feeling soon disappears. If it did not, you would find wearing clothes very itchy.

Find Out More

Outer covering
14–15

Skin deep
16–17

Communication

People communicate with each other in different ways. Speech allows you to communicate thoughts, ideas and feelings clearly to other people. Humans are the only animals that can do this. Through body language you can communicate without using words.

△ This woman is using sign language to communicate with children who have hearing difficulties. Each position and movement of her fingers and hands means a certain word.

Making sounds

You make sounds using your larynx (voice box). You can feel this by touching the bumpy part in your neck. If you speak or sing, you will feel your larynx vibrate as it produces sounds. Sounds are turned into speech by your tongue and lips. Push your tongue to the roof of your mouth and try speaking normally.

▽ Look at these children and their body language. The boy and girl facing one other appear interested in what each other is saying. The other boy is being left out.

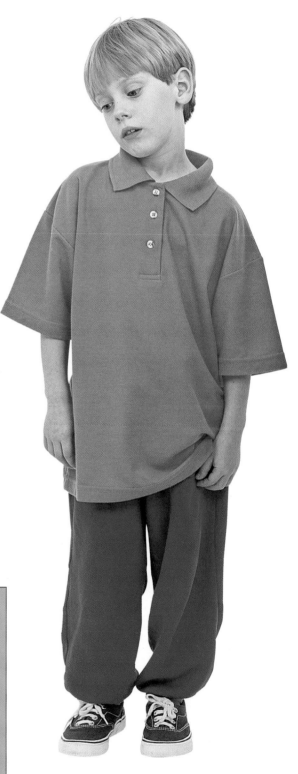

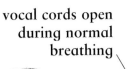

vocal cords open
during normal
breathing

vocal cords
shut during
speech

△ Stretched across the larynx are two folds called
vocal cords. Air forced between them as you breathe
out makes the vocal cords vibrate and make sounds.

△ When you speak your brain instructs
your tongue and lips to move and change
shape in order to form the words.

▷ What does this
pair's body language
tell you? The boy is
making a point
forcefully, as you
can see from his
fingers pointing.
The girl is being
defensive and is
showing it by
folding her arms
across her chest.

Find Out More

Learning
38–39

Touch
50–51

Hormones

Hormones are chemical messengers. They are produced by organs called endocrine (or hormonal) glands and are released into the bloodstream. Hormones control many body processes. For example, growth hormones make children grow and sex hormones enable people to reproduce and have babies.

▽ Look at the fear and excitement on the faces of the people on this scary rollercoaster ride. In a situation like this, your adrenal glands release the hormone adrenaline. It speeds up your heart and breathing rate so you are ready to face danger – or run away from it.

◁ Growth hormones make your body grow during childhood. This is why the teenager on the left is much taller than the child on the right.

△ Male sex hormones make hair grow on men's faces.

△ This girl has diabetes. Her pancreas does not produce enough of the hormone insulin, which provides energy-giving glucose. She has an insulin injection every day.

pituitary gland releases over nine hormones

thyroid gland releases two hormones

testes

thymus gland helps to fight infection

adrenal gland

pancreas

ovaries

◁ These are the main endocrine glands. Ovaries release sex hormones that make women look female. Testes release sex hormones that make men look male.

Find Out More

Egg and sperm 78–79

Growing up 84–85

Blood vessels

Blood vessels are the tubes that carry blood around your body to keep it alive. There are three types of blood vessel. Arteries carry oxygen-rich blood away from your heart. Veins carry oxygen-poor blood back to your heart. Millions of tiny capillaries link the arteries and veins and supply each individual cell with food and oxygen.

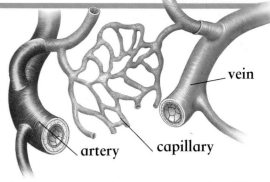

vein

artery   capillary

△ Arteries and veins are linked by a vast network of capillaries. Arteries divide to form the capillaries, which take blood close to the body cells and then join up to form veins.

rest of body   heart   lungs

△ Your body's system of blood vessels has two parts. One carries blood from the heart to the lungs to pick up oxygen. The other carries blood from the heart to all the other body parts to deliver oxygen.

▷ Here you can see the body's main veins. These carry blood from all parts of the body back to your heart. Veins from the legs and abdomen empty into a single large vein that runs up to the heart. Another large vein delivers blood from the head, chest and arms. Special pulmonary veins carry oxygen-rich blood from the lungs round to the left side of the heart.

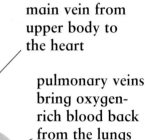

main vein from upper body to the heart

pulmonary veins bring oxygen-rich blood back from the lungs

heart

main vein from lower body

this vein carries blood back from the leg

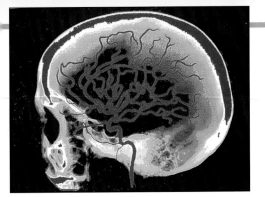

△ This X-ray of the head shows the branching carotid artery. The carotid arteries supply blood to your brain.

Measuring your pulse

Use two fingertips to feel the inside of your wrist, just below your thumb. Can you feel your pulse? This is caused by an artery under the skin bulging out when your heart beats. Count the number of pulse beats in 10 seconds. Ask a friend to time you. Multiply the number by six. This is your number of heart beats each minute.

pulmonary arteries take oxygen-poor blood to the lungs

the main artery leaving the heart

heart

this artery supplies the leg with blood

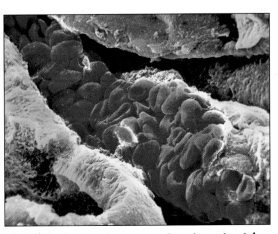

△ This is a microscopic view inside a tiny capillary. You can see a mass of densely packed red blood cells travelling through it. Capillaries pass very close to body cells. As this happens, the red blood cells give up their oxygen load to the cells.

◁ This shows the body's main arteries, carrying blood from the heart to all parts of the body. The biggest artery leaves the left side of the heart and sends branches to the head, arms, chest and legs. As arteries branch, they get smaller until they become capillaries. Special pulmonary arteries carry oxygen-poor blood from the heart to the lungs.

Find Out More

Living liquid
60–61

How you breathe
66–67

59

Living liquid

Blood is your body's liquid delivery and removal service. It is made up of four parts. Plasma delivers food to all your body's cells, while platelets help to heal wounds. Red blood cells carry oxygen to your cells and remove their waste. White blood cells play a vital part in your body's defence against germs.

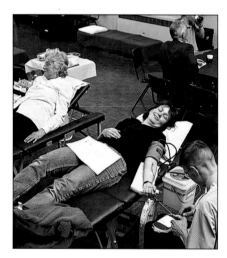

▷ This woman is giving blood. A needle is inserted into a vein in her arm and about half a litre of blood is collected. Her blood will later be given to someone who has lost blood in an accident or in an operation.

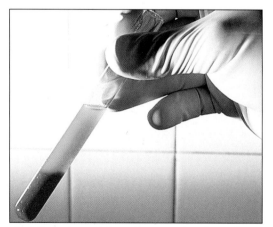

△ This is a blood sample that has been separated into its two main parts. Red blood cells are at the bottom and plasma is on top.

▽ A torrent of blood cascades along a tiny blood vessel. Floating in the yellowish liquid plasma is a mass of blood cells. In every drop of blood there are over 250 million red blood cells, 375,000 white blood cells, and 16 million platelets. Between four and six litres of blood flow around the body of an adult.

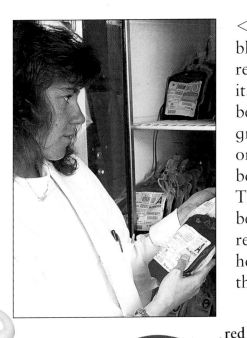

◁ When people give blood it is kept in a refrigerator to preserve it. Each person's blood belongs to one of four groups called A, B, AB or O. A label on each bag identifies the group. This is very important because the person who receives the blood must have the same group as the person who gave it.

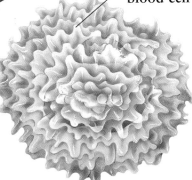

red blood cell

platelet

white blood cell

△ Doughnut-shaped red blood cells take oxygen from your lungs to the rest of the body. White blood cells find and destroy germs that might do harm. Platelets help to seal leaks in blood vessels.

Find Out More

Blood vessels
58–59

Infection
62–63

Infection

Germs, such as bacteria and viruses, are always trying to get inside your body. If they do, they can infect you and cause disease. Luckily, your body has many defences. Skin forms a barrier against germs, but if some manage to get through, white blood cells hunt them down and destroy them.

▽ A white blood cell called a 'cell-eater' has tracked down its prey. This is a germ that is attempting to infect the human body and cause disease. The cell-eater wraps itself round the germ, and destroys the germ by digesting it.

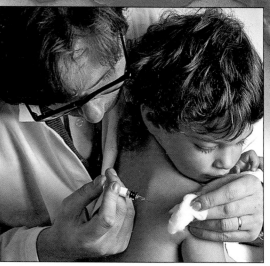

white
blood cell

△ This is a microscopic view of bacteria on the surface of the skin. These germs are harmless on the skin, but if they get inside your body, through cuts or down the throat, they infect you and cause disease.

◁ The heat-sensitive thermometer strip on this boy's head shows his body temperature. It should be about 37°C. If it is higher he may be ill. The body uses high temperature to kill germs. A very high temperature is called a fever.

△ A doctor injects a boy with a vaccine to protect him from a particular germ. The vaccine makes his body produce special chemicals to kill the germ if it attacks him.

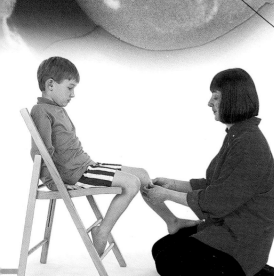

◁ Cut skin lets in germs. If you cut your skin, the body acts quickly to seal broken blood vessels and repair the damage. The blood clots, or thickens, and then dries to leave a scab like this one. Under the scab the healing process continues until the skin is repaired.

platelet net   red blood cells

▷ When a cut in the skin breaks a blood vessel, platelets in the blood form a 'net' that traps red blood cells.

clot   scab

▷ The trapped red blood cells make a clot that plugs the wound. The surface of the clot hardens to form a scab.

old scab

▷ Beneath the scab, the skin and the blood vessel repair themselves. At last, the old dry scab drops off.

invading germ

◁ This boy has grazed his knee. His mother washes the wound with cotton wool soaked in antiseptic liquid. This removes dirt and kills germs, so there is less chance they will invade the body.

Find Out More

Skin deep
16–17

Living liquid
60–61

Why you breathe

You need to breathe in air because it contains oxygen. Every cell in your body uses oxygen to release the energy from food that keeps your cells (and you!) alive. Oxygen is taken from the air by your breathing system – your nose, throat, windpipe and lungs. Inside the lungs, oxygen passes into the blood.

▷ The two lungs in your chest are linked to the outside by the windpipe. This opens into your throat. Lungs are soft and spongy, because they are made of a mass of tubes and tiny air bags. Blood flows through them constantly to pick up oxygen.

windpipe

right lung

△ In water there is little oxygen, and your lungs cannot work properly. To stop your body running out of oxygen if you go diving you have to carry your own air supply in tanks, like this woman swimming along a coral reef.

Catch your breath

Take a mirror and hold it just in front of your mouth. Now breathe out onto the surface of the mirror. What happens? You should find that a fine mist of water droplets has formed on the mirror. The insides of your lungs are moist. When you breathe out, the moist air forms the tiny droplets on the mirror.

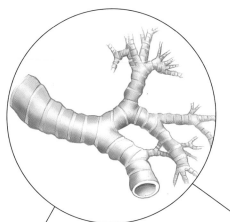

◁ Large tubes in your lungs branch again and again, getting narrower and narrower all the time. They eventually form tiny tubes no wider than a strand of hair.

▷ At the ends of the narrowest tubes are clusters of alveoli, tiny bags that look like bunches of grapes. These bags are where oxygen is taken into the blood. There are over 300 million of these bags in your lungs.

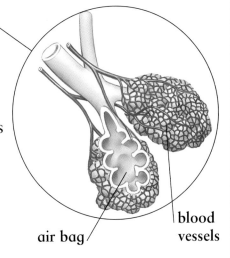

air bag

blood vessels

tubes

left lung

△ This cast of the inside of human lungs shows how the windpipe branches into many thousands of much smaller tubes.

Find Out More

How you breathe 66–67

Breathing trouble 68–69

Breathing trouble

Most of the time you breathe in and out regularly. Sometimes this is interrupted, by sneezes, yawns, coughs or hiccups. When you sneeze, air rushes from your lungs and bursts out through your nose to clear away any irritations. The droplets released by sneezing can pass disease from one person to another.

▽ When you sneeze, a jet of droplets shoots out of your nose and mouth, faster than a speeding car. Sneezes are triggered by dust, pollen or by the sticky mucus produced when you get a cold. Air from the lungs builds up in the windpipe and is then released to blast out the irritation.

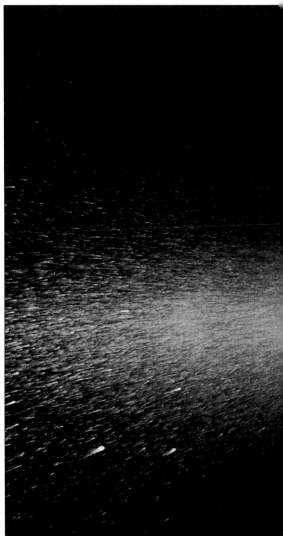

◁ Like many people, this girl suffers from hayfever in the summer months. She is sensitive to pollen grains that she has breathed in. The pollen irritates her, and gives her a sore throat, sore eyes and a runny nose.

▷ This is a microscopic view of pollen grains. Millions of grains are produced by flowers in order to reproduce. Pollen grains cause hayfever when they are breathed in by certain people.

▷ This boy has asthma and is using an inhaler. Asthma makes it difficult to breathe because the small tubes in the lungs suddenly get narrower. The drug from the inhaler makes the tubes wider.

◁ Pollution means that something is added to your surroundings that should not be there. In the modern world, pollution of the air you breathe is caused by gases and tiny dust particles released from factories and cars. This pollution may be the reason why more and more people are developing asthma and other breathing diseases.

△ These are human lungs. The top picture shows the lungs of a person who never smoked. The bottom picture shows the lungs of a heavy smoker who died of lung cancer. The black marks are produced by cigarette smoke. Cigarettes are the main cause of lung cancer.

◁ When you yawn, you open your mouth wide and take an extra deep breath in and out of your lungs. You breathe less deeply than normal when you are tired, so waste carbon dioxide builds up inside your lungs. Yawning drives out the stale air from your body.

Find Out More

Why you breathe
64–65

When you are ill
94–95

Why you eat

Just as a car needs petrol to keep moving, you need food to keep your body working properly. Food contains useful substances called nutrients. Nutrients provide energy and building materials for growth and repair. For you to use these nutrients, your food must first be digested, or broken down into smaller pieces.

◁ Food provides you with the energy needed to do activities such as tennis, dancing, swimming and walking. Nutrients rich in energy are used by your muscles to make them contract and move your body.

◁ Nearly two-thirds of your body is made up of water. You lose water when you go to the toilet or sweat. Lost water has to be replaced. You take in water when you drink and when you eat.

Digesting bread

Take a piece of bread and put it in your mouth. Chew it for a few minutes before swallowing it. At first the bread has little taste, but after some chewing it tastes sweet. This is because the saliva (spit) inside your mouth contains an enzyme (digesting chemical). It digests the starch in bread by turning it into sweet sugars.

△ Whether you are lying down or standing up, fast asleep or wide awake, your body is constantly making use of the food you eat and digest. After being digested, food is carried to all your body cells by blood. As nutrients are used up by the cells, your brain detects that levels of nutrients in your blood are getting less. When this happens you start to feel hungry and eat more food.

◁ From the time you are born until your body is growing. The various nutrients in food play different roles in the growing process. Some act as the building blocks which are used to make your muscles, bones and other body parts bigger. Others provide the constant supply of energy needed to make you grow. To make sure you grow properly it is important to eat a mixed, healthy diet.

△ Your body is constantly repairing itself. Its ability to do this becomes obvious if you break your arm. The bones in your arm rebuild themselves. All these repair processes need nutrients from the food you eat.

◁ This food blender illustrates what happens to food during digestion. On the left, the blender contains bite-size chunks of food. On the right, the blender has broken down the food chunks into a soup.

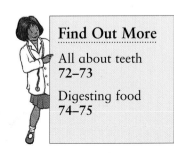

Find Out More

All about teeth
72–73

Digesting food
74–75

71

All about teeth

Your teeth cut and crush food into small pieces so it can be swallowed and digested. There are four main types of teeth. Incisors slide past each other to cut up food. Pointed canines grip and pierce food, and flat-topped premolars and molars crush food. During a lifetime, a person has two sets of teeth – milk teeth and adult teeth.

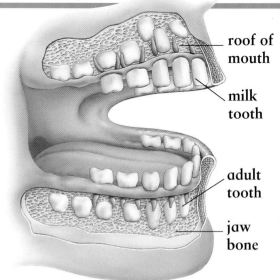

roof of mouth

milk tooth

adult tooth

jaw bone

△ During childhood, your 20 milk teeth are pushed out of your gums and replaced by adult teeth.

premolar

molar

wisdom tooth

◁ This wide-open mou reveals a full set of adu teeth. Altogether there a 32 teeth – eight incisor four canines, eight premolars and 12 mola Although most adult tee appear by the age of 1 the back molar teeth (wisdom teeth) appear when you are an adult.

canine

incisor

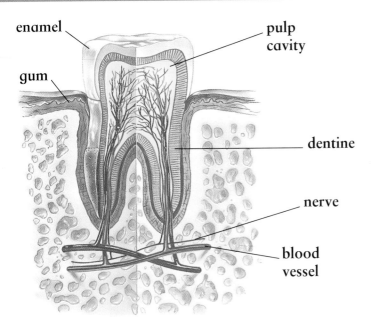

enamel

pulp cavity

gum

dentine

nerve

blood vessel

△ A tooth has a covering of hard, white enamel. Inside, a bony dentine layer surrounds the inner pulp cavity with its blood vessels and nerve endings.

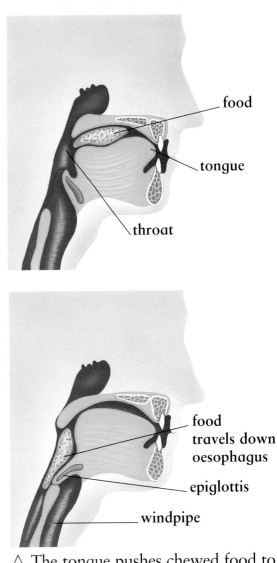

food

tongue

throat

food travels down oesophagus

epiglottis

windpipe

△ The tongue pushes chewed food to the back of your throat and sets off the automatic process of swallowing. A flap called the epiglottis covers your windpipe as you swallow. This stops food going down 'the wrong way' and making you choke.

▷ It is important to clean your teeth thoroughly two or three times each day. Brushing removes leftover food and helps prevent tooth decay.

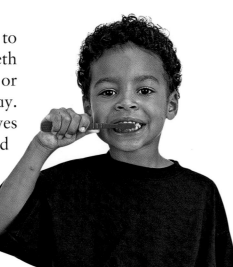

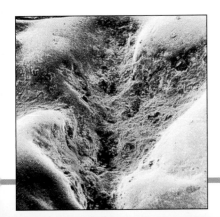

◁ This molar is covered with plaque, a mixture of food and bacteria which builds up if teeth are not cleaned. It releases acids that cause tooth decay.

Find Out More

Why you eat 70–71

Digesting food 74–75

Digesting food

Before your body can use the food you eat, it needs to digest it – break it down into simple nutrients. Food is crushed to a paste in your stomach, and then digested in your small intestine by special chemicals called enzymes. The nutrients pass through the wall of the small intestine into your blood. Any waste matter travels along your large intestine and out through your anus.

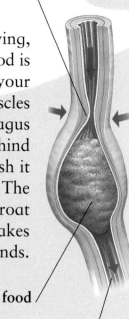

muscles contract

▷ After swallowing, the chewed food is squeezed down your oesophagus. Muscles in the oesophagus wall contract behind the food to push it downwards. The journey from throat to stomach takes about five seconds.

food

oesophagus

liver

large intestine

small intestine

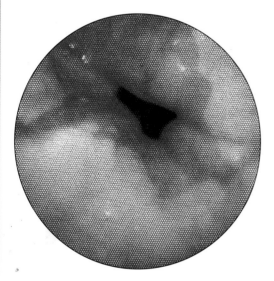

◁ The oesophagus connects your mouth to your stomach. This view of the oesophagus at the stomach entrance is produced using an instrument called an endoscope. The walls of the oesophagus are shiny and slimy so that food can slip down easily.

Food journey

Take a long sock and put a tennis ball inside one end of it. Hold the end of the sock with one hand and grip the sock just behind the ball with the other. Now squeeze with your fingers to push the ball so it slides along the sock. This action is similar to what happens when food travels down your oesophagus.

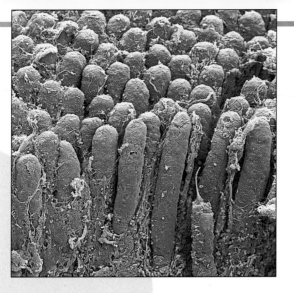

◁ This microscopic view inside the small intestine looks like a forest of little fingers. These 'fingers' are called villi, and each one is about one millimetre long. Nutrients from digested food pass through these villi in the small intestine to your bloodstream.

oesophagus

▷ Inside your large intestine there are millions of germs called bacteria. Normally they are harmless, but if you get the bacteria on your fingers and then touch your food, they can make you ill. That is why it is important to wash your hands after going to the toilet.

stomach

pancreas

◁ When you need to get rid of waste matter (faeces), you go to the toilet. Babies cannot control when they release faeces so they need to wear a nappy that is changed regularly.

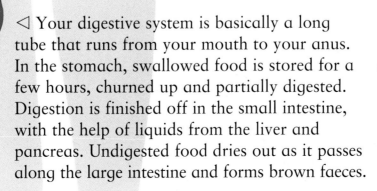

◁ Your digestive system is basically a long tube that runs from your mouth to your anus. In the stomach, swallowed food is stored for a few hours, churned up and partially digested. Digestion is finished off in the small intestine, with the help of liquids from the liver and pancreas. Undigested food dries out as it passes along the large intestine and forms brown faeces.

rectum

anus

Find Out More

Why you eat
70–71

All about teeth
72–73

Waste disposal

Millions of chemical processes go on inside your body's cells. These processes release wastes into your blood which would poison you if you did not get rid of them. The job of disposing of this waste is carried out by the urinary system which filters waste and surplus water from your blood to make urine. The urine is released when you go to the toilet.

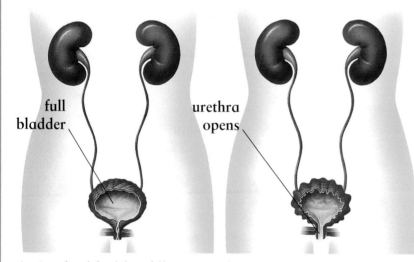

full bladder

urethra opens

artery

vein

ureter

△ As the bladder fills, it sends messages to the brain so that you feel a need to go to the toilet. The muscles at the bottom of the bladder relax, making the urethra open, and the bladder walls contract to squeeze out the urine.

Kidney sieve

Mix together some salt and sugar and shake it in a sieve over a bowl. The salt passes through the sieve while the sugar stays in it. Your kidneys 'sieve' blood so that you lose waste but keep nutrients.

◁ The kidney has three main parts – the cortex, medulla and pelvis. Blood enters through an artery, which branches into many tiny capillaries, and leaves through a vein. In the cortex and medulla there are about one million tiny filtering units called nephrons. Each nephron filters blood. It removes waste and surplus water from the blood to make urine. The urine then collects in the pelvis before trickling down the ureter to the bladder.

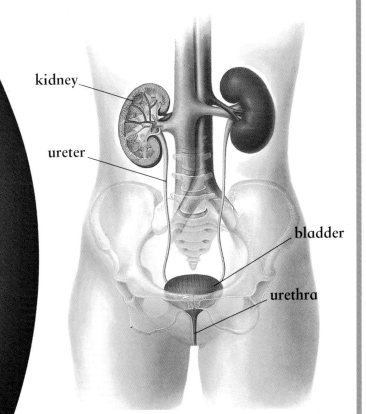

kidney

ureter

bladder

urethra

△ The urinary system consists of the two kidneys, the two ureters, the bladder and the urethra. The bean-shaped kidneys are on either side of the backbone, behind your stomach. In girls, the opening of the urethra is between their legs. In boys, it opens at the end of the penis.

cortex of kidney

medulla of kidney

pelvis of kidney

Find Out More

Why you eat
70–71

Digesting food
74–75

Egg and sperm

Adult humans use their reproductive systems to make babies. Males produce cells called sperm that can swim. Females produce a single egg each month. To make a baby, a man puts his penis inside a woman's vagina to release sperm. The sperm swim towards the egg and fertilize it. The fertilized egg grows into a baby inside the uterus.

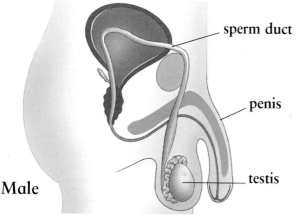

Male

sperm duct

penis

testis

△ Millions of sperm are made in the testes every day. They travel along the sperm duct and out through the penis.

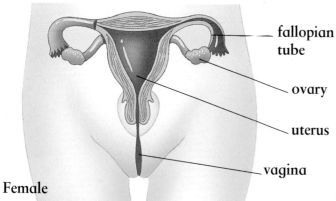

fallopian tube

ovary

uterus

vagina

Female

△ The ovaries release an egg each month. An egg is fertilized if it meets a sperm as it travels along a fallopian tube to the uterus.

△ A mass of sperm surrounds an egg as it travels along the fallopian tube. Each sperm tries to break through the outer layer of the egg to fertilize it. They all release chemicals to dissolve the outer layer. Only one sperm will manage to get through.

◁ This sperm is breaking through the covering of the egg. As soon as the sperm gets inside, the egg produces a chemical barrier that stops any other sperm entering. Inside the egg, the sperm's tail drops off. The nucleus of the sperm (inside its head) joins with the nucleus of the egg and fertilizes it.

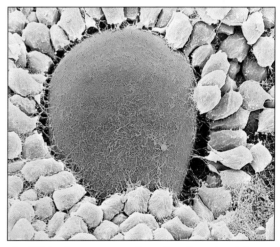

△ This is an egg developing inside an ovary. Each egg grows inside a small bag called a follicle. Here, you can see blue follicle cells around the egg. These cells feed and protect the egg as it develops. When it is ready, the follicle bursts open and the egg floats out into the fallopian tube.

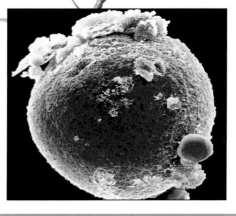

▷ This is a microscopic view of an egg that has just been released from the ovary and is travelling along the fallopian tube. It is 0.1 mm across. Around it are pieces of the follicle.

Find Out More

A new life
80–81

All about babies
82–83

79

A new life

If a sperm fertilizes an egg inside a woman a new life is produced. The fertilized egg divides to produce a hollow ball of cells that settles in the uterus. Over the next nine months, this ball of cells will develop into a baby. The developing baby is linked to its mother by the umbilical cord. Food and oxygen pass from the mother to the baby along the cord.

wall of uterus

fully-formed foetus

egg is fertilized here

uterus

fertilized egg settles in uterus wall

position of uterus

△ A fertilized egg divides again and again as it travels towards the uterus. After about seven days, it arrives in the uterus and settles into its soft lining.

membrane

protective fluid

▷ Two days after fertilization, the single cell of the fertilized egg has divided to become four cells. These cells will carry on dividing until they become the billions of cells that make a human body.

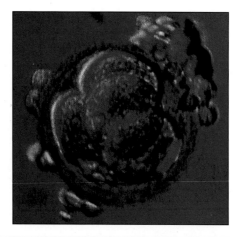

▷ This baby is between 38 and 40 weeks old, and is ready to be born. Some weeks earlier it turned upside down, so it will be born head first. During birth the muscular wall of the uterus starts to contract. The membrane around the baby breaks, and the uterus squeezes the baby outside through the vagina.

◁ At five weeks old, the baby is about the size of an apple pip. It has a tail which will soon disappear. Buds are forming that will become the arms and legs, and the heart is just starting to beat.

▷ At eight weeks old, the developing baby is called a foetus. It is as big as a strawberry. You can see its eyes, ears and tiny developing fingers and toes.

umbilical cord

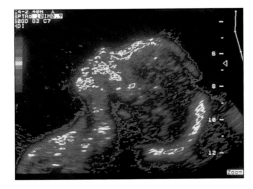

◁ This ultrasound scan of a woman's uterus shows a 22-week-old foetus. You can see its head and face clearly. Doctors use ultrasound scans as a safe way of checking that the foetus is healthy.

▷ This woman is pregnant. That means that she is expecting a baby. You can tell she is pregnant because the growing foetus inside her uterus is making her abdomen bulge outwards.

vagina

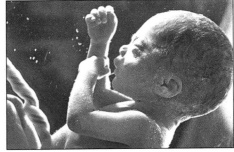

△ This baby has just been born and taken her first breath. She is still attached to her umbilical cord.

Find Out More

All about babies
82–83

Growing up
84–85

Growing up

Everyone grows up in the same way. During the first year after birth, the body grows very quickly. Through the rest of childhood, growth is slow and steady, as children develop the skills that they will need as adults. Finally, in the early teens, growth speeds up again as children become adults. As adults, men and women no longer grow.

◁ At nearly one year old, this infant can sit up, crawl and pull himself onto his feet by holding onto a chair. His head is still quite large compared to the rest of his body.

▷ This two-year-old child is busy learning by playing with some coloured plastic shapes. She is able to walk and climb stairs and is learning to talk. She can also draw simple pictures.

◁ This eight-year-old can ride a bicycle and perform many other skilled actions. The child is able to read and write clearly and accurately, and speak using a wide range of words.

◁ These two teenagers have reached puberty. This is a time of rapid growth when children start to look like adult men and women. It is also the time when their reproductive systems start working, so they can have children. Puberty usually happens between the ages of about 10 and 16 and begins earlier in girls than boys. At the age of 20 growth comes to an end.

◁ In their 20s and 30s many men and women get married and have children. They now have to spend much of their time looking after their children, and will continue to do so until the children leave home.

▷ By their 40s and 50s, most men and women show signs of getting older. Very slowly, their bodies become less efficient at doing things.

△ As people get older, their skin wrinkles, their hair turns grey and their bodies become less strong.

Find Out More

Family tree 86–87

Similarities 88–89

Family tree

In every family, there are similarities between parents and their children. This is because when men and women have children, they pass on tiny packages of information called chromosomes in their egg and sperm. These are instructions that will make a unique new person, who will have some of the features of both parents, as well as many of his or her own.

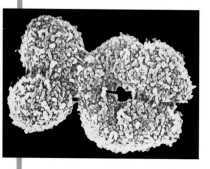

◁ This is one of the chromosomes found inside each of your body's cells. Chromosomes carry information that controls the features of your body, such as the colour of your eyes.

▷ These girls are identical twins. Their cells contain identical chromosomes. When their mother's egg was fertilized, it split into two halves, and each developed into a girl.

Make a family tree

Collect photographs of yourself, your parents, any brothers or sisters, grandparents and even great-grandparents. Now arrange them on the page with you at the bottom, your parents above you, and your grandparents above them. Look at the photos. Can you see any similarities that have been 'passed on' from one generation to the next?

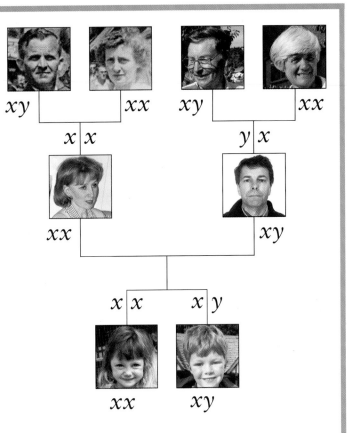

xy xx xy xx

$x \mid x$ $y \mid x$

xx xy

$x \mid x$ $x \mid y$

xx xy

△ Two of the chromosomes inside each of your cells control whether you are a girl or a boy. They are called the sex chromosomes. There are two types, X and Y. Boys have one X and one Y chromosome, while girls have two X chromosomes. A man's sperm can carry either an X or a Y chromosome, but a woman's egg can only contain an X chromosome. If an X-carrying sperm fertilizes an egg, a girl (XX) is produced. If a Y-carrying sperm fertilizes the egg, a boy (XY) is produced.

◁ Here are three generations of one family. The man on the left is the father of the woman, and grandfather of the two children. The children's father is standing on the right. See if you can spot any similarities between the generations.

Find Out More

Egg and sperm
78–79

Similarities
88–89

Similarities

Look at people in the street, and you will notice many differences. But look again and see if you can spot the similarities – such as the way people shrug their shoulders, frown when they are thinking, wave goodbye or laugh at your jokes. You will see behaviour like this all round the world.

▽ A crowd of children play in a playground in Cuba. Although they all move, shout and laugh in exactly the same way as you, each child has their own personality. Some are girls and some are boys. Some have lighter skin and some have darker skin, and they might be speaking in a different language to you. These differences add variety and interest to all our lives.

▷ Find a photo of yourself and stick it here with glue. You have taken your place in this gallery of human beings!

Your
photograph
goes here

◁ This boy is unable to walk and must use a wheelchair to get around – and do his homework in! Having this, or any other disability, should not stop people living their lives to the full.

◁ These athletes race in their high-speed wheelchairs with the same urge to win as able-bodied athletes. We all have the same ability to succeed, if given an opportunity.

◁ These children are playing in a back street in Morocco. All children play, whether they live in a city or a village in the middle of a rainforest. Playing with other children allows a child to practise the skills they will need when they grow up.

▷ This is a child from Nepal in the foothills of the Himalayas. His skin colour and the shape of his face may differ from yours, but his smile is a sign of greeting and of happiness that would be recognized anywhere in the world.

△ People everywhere enjoy playing games. These Brazilian boys do not own a draught set, so they use bottle tops instead.

◁ Two Australian girls go walking in the afternoon sun. The one with darker hair and skin has greater natural protection from the harmful effects of strong sunlight.

Find Out More

Our bodies
10–11

Growing up
84–85

89

Healthy food

Food is made up of nutrients which give your body the energy you need to move, and the building materials that make you grow. You need a variety of these nutrients to help keep you fit and healthy. This is called a balanced diet. The food pyramid shows what to eat to get the balance right.

▷ Fats keep you warm, but you should only eat a small amount. They are at the top of the food pyramid because you need less of them than other foods.

▷ Dairy products, such as milk, provide calcium which is needed for strong teeth and bones. Milk is healthier than a glass of sugary cola.

▷ Food rich in proteins is essential for the body to grow and repair itself. Beans, fish, chicken, meat and cheese are all good sources of protein. Meat and cheese also contain a lot of fat.

▷ Fresh fruit and vegetables provide you with fibre, as well as plenty of vitamins and minerals. Fibre keeps your digestion working smoothly. Vitamins and minerals are essential for good health.

▷ Foods rich in carbohydrates should make up most of your diet. Rice, bread, potatoes and pasta are all rich in starchy carbohydrates. These release their energy slowly and keep you fuelled up through the day.

△ This meal is not well-balanced. It contains a lot of fat and salt, and hardly any fibre or vitamins.

Keep a food diary
Try keeping a food diary to see whether you are eating a balanced diet or not. For two days, write down everthing you eat at each meal. Using the food pyramid, write down beside each meal what nutrients it contains. Are your meals balanced, or do they contain lots of fats and sugar? Use your diary to think about how you might improve your diet.

◁ A baked potato is a good source of energy because it is packed with starchy carbohydrates. Unlike chips, which are potatoes fried in oil, baked potatoes contain little fat.

▷ This vegetable curry is a balanced meal. Rice provides plenty of carbohydrates, the vegetables give you fibre, vitamins and minerals, the lentils contain protein, and the sauce a little fat.

Find Out More

Why you eat
70–71

Digesting food
74–75

93

When you are ill

Sometimes parts of the body stop working properly and you become ill. This may happen because the body becomes infected by germs from outside, or because something is damaged inside the body. Doctors conduct tests and use their knowledge and experience to work out what is wrong with their patients.

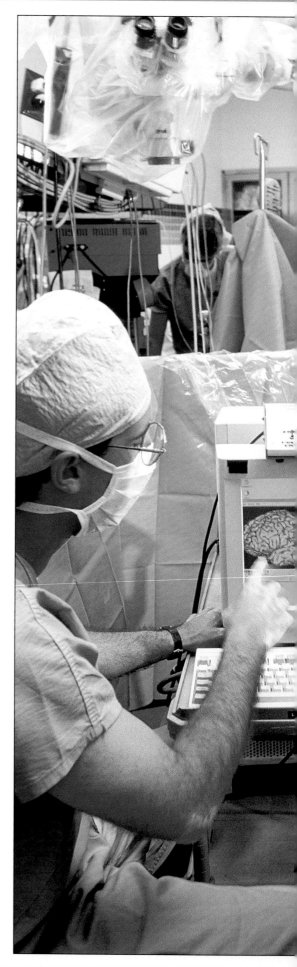

◁ This girl has a clinical thermometer in her mouth, under her tongue. It will stay there for a few minutes to measure the temperature inside her body. Normally this should be about 37°C. If she is ill her temperature may go up.

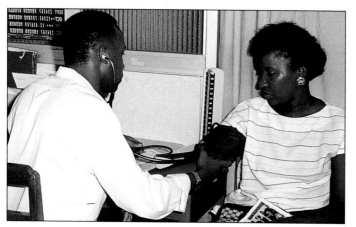

△ This doctor is measuring his patient's blood pressure. Blood pressure is produced by the heart when it beats. It measures how strongly blood is pushed along the arteries. If this woman's pressure is too high or too low, she may need treatment.

▷ This X-ray shows that the bones in the forearm are broken. X-rays allow doctors to 'look inside' a person's body. This patient's arm will be put in plaster to allow the bones to repair themselves properly.

◁ Wounds in the skin are usually covered with a dressing or bandage. This protects the wound from any bacteria in the air or on the skin that might get into the wound and infect it. It may also help to hold the wound together as it heals.

▷ Drugs may be taken to kill germs or to correct other problems inside the body. Pills and medicines are swallowed, but drugs may also be injected through the skin.

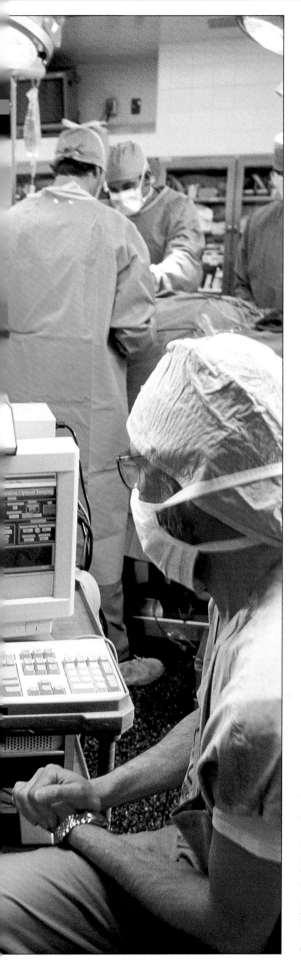

◁ Problems inside the body can require surgery in an operating theatre. The surgeon makes an opening in the body to repair the problem and then sews it up again. Here, a surgeon opens a person's skull to operate on the brain, while other doctors look at a scan of the problem area.

Find Out More

Our bodies
10–11

Infection
62–63

Spare parts

It is becoming increasingly possible to repair the body with artificial parts if something goes wrong. These parts include artificial limbs, false teeth, heart pacemakers and metal joints. Some scientists are trying to develop robots that will one day be able to behave exactly the same way as humans.

△ This Afghan boy had part of his right leg blown off when he stepped on a land-mine. He has been fitted with an artificial leg and is now trying to return to a normal life at a rehabilitation (recovery) centre.

◁ This robot has a shape that looks quite human, but it cannot copy all human activities as it does not have human intelligence.

▷ Computers are becoming more complex all the time, but no computer is as intelligent as a human brain.

▷ This girl does not have any artificial body parts. If she did need them, the body parts shown are all available today. By the time she is grown up, many more parts will have been developed to replace worn out or damaged areas of the body.

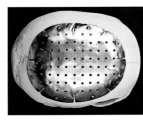

▷ A metal plate is screwed over a skull fracture to protect it as it heals.

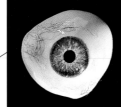

◁ Artificial eyes sometimes replace eyes that are diseased or damaged.

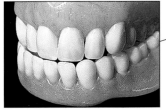

△ False teeth, or dentures, are fitted for patients whose teeth have been removed or have fallen out.

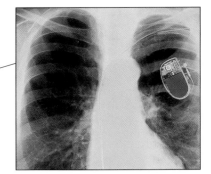

△ A heart pacemaker sends electrical signals to the heart to keep it beating at a regular rate.

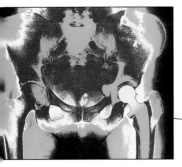

△ This X-ray shows a metal hip joint. The diseased joint is replaced to help the patient walk properly.

△ This man has an artificial forearm. Signals from the muscles in the upper arm allow the hand to move and grip.

▷ This artificial leg is used when a person's leg has been amputated. The leg has a cup into which the stump of the leg fits, and joints at the 'knee' and 'ankle' to make it flexible.

Find Out More

Bones and joints 24–25

Control centre 34–35

Amazing facts

Everything about the human body is incredible. There are hundreds of amazing facts and records about everything in your body, from your smallest cells to your largest organs. You will have read about many of these in the encyclopedia, but here are a few more really astounding facts.

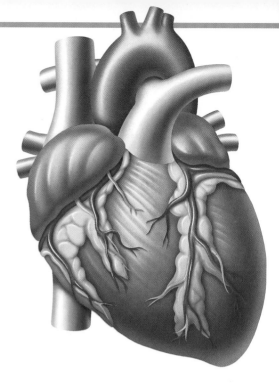

Blueprint for life
• Most of the body's 50 million million million cells contain 46 sets of instructions called chromosomes that run the cell and build a human body.
• Individual instructions in the chromosome are called genes. There are over 100,000 genes in each cell.

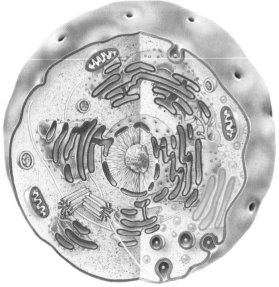

Shelf life
• Some cells live for a matter of days, while others last for years. In most cases, lost cells are replaced instantly.
• Cells lining the small intestine survive for three to six days before being worn away.

• Cells in the epidermis of the skin live for about 25 days before flaking off. About 36 million are lost every day.
• Red blood cells live for about 120 days.
• Liver cells live for about 500 days.
• Bone cells live for many years.
• Many nerve cells survive for a lifetime, although the brain loses about 1,000 cells each day which are not replaced. (Don't worry, this doesn't make you any less brainy!)

Mass production
• Some types of body cells are produced in huge numbers every day.
• To carry oxygen around the body, 170 billion red blood cells are produced daily.
• To fight disease, 10 billion white blood cells are produced daily.
• In a man's testes, 300 million sperm are produced every day.

Spaghetti junction
• Stood on its end, the stretched-out digestive system would be more than three times the height of an adult.
• The longest part of the digestive system is the small intestine which is about five metres long – longer than a car.

Nail facts
- Fingernails grow about 5 mm each month.
- Your fingernails grow four times faster than your toenails.
- Both fingernails and toenails grow faster in summer than in winter.
- The fingernails on your dominant hand (depending on whether you are right-handed or left-handed) grow slightly faster than the fingernails on the other hand.

Nervous information
- Nerve cells, or neurons, are the longest cells in the body and can reach up to one metre in length.
- Electrical nerve impulses can travel along neurons at up to 400 kilometres per hour.
- Laid end to end, the nerves in your body would stretch for an incredible 75 kilometres!

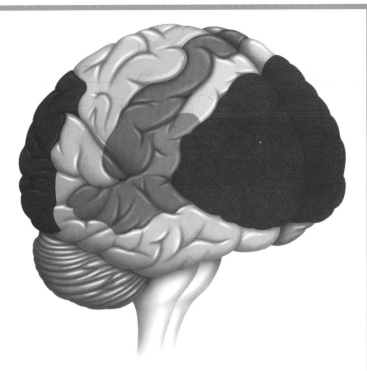

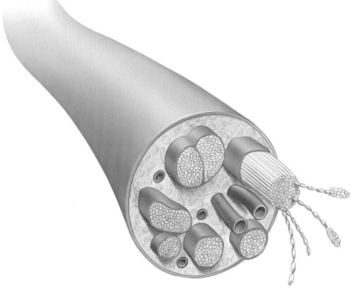

Brain power
- Your remarkable brain contains over 100 million million nerve cells.
- Keeping your brain working needs a colossal amount of oxygen and glucose to give it energy.
- Although the brain weighs just 2 per cent of your body weight, it uses 20 per cent of your body's oxygen, 20 per cent of its fuel supply and 15 per cent of its blood.

Gas exchanges
- Every day you breathe in and out about 25,000 times, with about 12,500 litres of air travelling through your lungs.
- Everyone releases up to two litres of gas, called flatus or farts, through their anus every day – enough to fill a party balloon!

Hairy stories
- Your hair grows about 1.2 cm every month.
- If hair is not cut, it usually stops growing when it gets to about 60 cm long.
- Some women can grow their hair very long indeed. The record length was nearly four metres!

Life records
- The average height of adult women is 1.65 metres and for adult men it is 1.78 metres. In some parts of the world, children are growing to be much taller than their parents, because they have a better, more nutritious diet when they are young.
- In a normal lifetime, an average person eats 30 tonnes of food, produces 35,770 litres of urine, and has 152,000,000 litres of blood pumped round their body!

Body quiz

How much do you know about the human body? Try these questions to test your knowledge. The answers are all to be found somewhere in the encyclopedia (and also on page 103).

TRUE OR FALSE?

1. Watching TV is better exercise than walking.

True or False?

2. The left side of your brain controls the right side of your body.

True or False?

3. Sweating helps to keep your body warm.

True or False?

4. Identical twins have identical fingerprints.

True or False?

5. Neuron is another name for a nerve cell.

True or False?

6. You only produce tears when you are crying.

True or False?

7. Reflex actions, like blinking, happen without you thinking about them.

True or False?

8. You have millions of harmless germs inside your body.

True or False?

9. White blood cells carry oxygen around the body.

True or False?

10. Arteries are blood vessels that carry blood towards the heart.

True or False?

11. Your sense of taste is 10,000 times more sensitive than your sense of smell.

True or False?

12. Light is detected in the eyes by sensors called rods and cones.

True or False?

13. Babies can walk when they are six months old.

True or False?

14. Chicken and fish are two foods that are rich in fibre.

True or False?

15. You have an anvil, a stirrup and a hammer in your body.

True or False?

16. Water makes up about one quarter of your body's weight.

True or False?

WHICH ANSWER CORRECTLY COMPLETES EACH STATEMENT?

1. The clear part at the front of your eye is called the:

a) carina.
b) corona.
c) cornea.

2. Your lungs are spongy because they are filled with millions of tiny air bags called:

a) alveoli.
b) ravioli.
c) aioli.

3. Your heart beats to pump blood around the body:

a) all the time, at the same rate whatever you are doing.
b) all the time, but speeds up when you exercise.
c) during the day, but stops at night for a rest.

4. Just over half of your balanced diet should be made up of:

a) starchy food such as rice, potatoes, bread or pasta.
b) protein foods such as poultry, fish, eggs and beans.
c) fatty foods such as dairy products, burgers and chips.

5. The waste liquid called urine that pours from your body when you go to the toilet is made in the:

a) stomach.
b) kidneys.
c) bladder.

6. The brown pigment that colours your skin and protects it from sunlight is called:

a) melanin.
b) melanie.
c) melamine.

7. You lose skin flakes from the surface of your skin all the time as your clothes rub against it. Each year you lose a total of:

a) four grammes of skin flakes.
b) four kilograms of skin flakes.
c) four tonnes of skin flakes.

8. The longest part of your digestive system is the:

a) large intestine.
b) oesophagus.
c) small intestine.

Glossary

A glossary is a kind of mini-dictionary. Its job is to describe and explain some of the more difficult words in the main part of this book. If you come across a word you do not understand, you will probably find it listed here. Next to the word, you will find an explanation of what it means. Just like a dictionary, the glossary is arranged in alphabetical order, from A to Z.

abdomen The lower part of the main body between your chest and your legs. The abdomen contains your stomach and other organs involved in digesting food, as well as your two kidneys and bladder.

alveoli Tiny air bags found in their millions inside your lungs. Oxygen passes from the air into your bloodstream through alveoli.

atrium The left atrium and right atrium are chambers in the upper part of the heart. 'Atria' is the word used to describe more than one atrium.

balanced diet Your diet describes what you eat. A balanced diet is one that gives your body a wide range of nutrients – carbohydrates, fats, proteins, vitamins and minerals – in the right amounts needed for good health.

blood vessel A tube that carries blood through the body. The main types of blood vessels are arteries, veins, and capillaries.

cancer A disease caused by cells dividing out of control. When they do this they produce growths called tumours that stop the body working properly. There are lots of different types of cancer, many of which can be treated by doctors.

carbohydrates These are nutrients that supply your body with energy. Foods rich in carbohydrates include pasta, potatoes and rice.

carbon dioxide A type of gas found in the air around you. When your cells, using oxygen, release energy from food they release carbon dioxide as waste. This is carried to the lungs and breathed out into the air.

cartilage A tough rubbery material. Cartilage supports parts of your body, such as your nose and ears. It also covers the ends of bones where they meet in joints.

cells Your body is made up of billions of these tiny living units. There are many different types of cells, each with their own job to do.

cerebrum The main part of your brain. The wrinkled cerebrum enables you to feel, think, speak and see, and it makes your body move.

chromosome X-shaped packages of information found inside every one of your body's cells. Chromosomes contain the instructions needed to build a living human being.

cochlea Part of the inner ear shaped like a snail's shell. The cochlea picks up sound waves and sends messages to the brain so that you can hear.

cranium The upper dome-shaped part of the skull that surrounds the brain and protects it from being damaged.

diabetes A disease caused by lack of a hormone called insulin, which is produced by the pancreas. Insulin makes sure there is enough glucose in your blood to give you energy. People with diabetes need to inject themselves with insulin to keep glucose levels normal.

diaphragm A sheet of muscle that separates your chest from your abdomen. Your diaphragm plays an important part in breathing.

digestion The process by which the food you eat is broken down into simple nutrients your body can use. Digestion takes place inside the digestive system.

enzyme A special substance that breaks down food into simple nutrients during digestion.

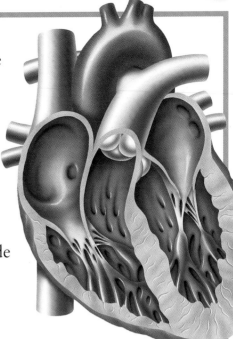

fats These are nutrients that are used to give you energy, and to help build your body. The fats are stored under the skin, to keep you warm. Foods rich in fats include milk and other dairy products, meat and eggs.

fertilization The joining together of an egg from a woman and a sperm from a man. A fertilized egg produced by fertilization grows and develops into a baby.

fibre Material found in plant foods such as fruits and beans. Although fibre is not digested, it is important because it makes digestion work efficiently.

foetus The name given to the baby developing inside its mother's uterus from eight weeks after fertilization until it is born.

hormones Chemical messengers produced by special glands such as the pituitary gland and pancreas. Hormones are carried by the blood to tell parts of your body what to do.

joint Part of the skeleton where two or more bones meet. Some joints, like those in the skull are fixed. Most are flexible and allow the body to move.

melanin Brown pigment (colouring) found in the skin that gives it colour and protects it from the harmful effects of sunlight. Melanin also colours people's hair.

minerals This is a group of nutrients needed in tiny amounts to make sure your body is working properly. Foods rich in minerals include fresh fruit and vegetables, cereals, nuts, fish and seafood, dairy products and meat.

muscle Part of the body that can contract (get shorter). Over 640 skeletal muscles (muscles attached to your bones) are controlled by your brain to pull bones and make your body move.

nephrons Tiny filtering units found inside your kidneys. Nephrons clean your blood by removing poisonous waste and surplus water to make urine.

neurons Nerve cells that make up your nervous system and carry electrical messages at high speed. Neurons have a thin, very long section called a nerve fibre that carries messages between your brain and all parts of your body. Nerve fibres are bundled together.

nucleus The control centre of every body cell. The nucleus contains 46 chromosomes that hold the instructions to build and operate that cell.

nutrients Substances contained in the food you eat that are needed to keep you alive. Nutrients supply your body with energy and the raw materials needed for growth and repair.

organ A major part of the body such as the brain, kidney or heart. Each organ carries out a specific job or jobs.

oxygen A type of gas found in the air. Oxygen is essential for life. You take it in through your lungs. Your cells use oxygen to release energy from food.

papillae Tiny bumps found on the surface of your tongue. Many papillae contain taste buds that detect tastes in food and drink.

plaque A deposit of bacteria and food that builds up on teeth if they are not cleaned properly. Bacteria in plaque release substances that cause tooth decay.

proteins These are nutrients used by your body for growth and repair. Foods rich in proteins include fish, chicken, meat and beans.

reflex An automatic action such as blinking, swallowing or pulling your hand away from a hot object, that you do without thinking about it.

skeleton Framework of 206 bones that supports your body, allows you to move and protects delicate organs such as your brain.

suture Joint between skull bones that does not allow movement. In a suture the bones are locked together like pieces in a jigsaw.

sweat A salty, waste liquid produced by the skin, especially when you are hot. When sweat evaporates (goes into the air) from your skin's surface, it draws heat from your body and cools you down.

system A group of organs that work together to do a particular job. The oesophagus, stomach and intestines, for example, make up the digestive system that digests your food.

tendon A tough cord that connects the end of a muscle to a bone. When the muscle contracts it pulls the bone through the tendon.

tissue A collection of cells of the same type that work together. Different tissues form an organ.

umbilical cord Cord containing blood vessels that links a foetus to its mother when it is growing inside her uterus. The umbilical cord carries food and oxygen to the foetus and removes its waste.

urine Waste liquid made inside the kidneys. Urine is stored in the bladder which empties every few hours when you go to the toilet.

vaccine A medicine given to a person, often by an injection, that helps to protect them against particular diseases.

ventricle One of the two lower chambers – right and left – of the heart. The right ventricle pumps blood to the lungs; the left pumps blood to the rest of the body.

villi Tiny finger-like projections that line the inside of your small intestine. Villi make sure that, after digestion, nutrients are taken into your bloodstream as quickly as possible.

vitamins This is a group of nutrients needed in small amounts by your body to make sure it works properly. Foods rich in vitamins include fresh fruit and vegetables, cereals, eggs, fish and meat.

Index

This index helps you find subjects in this book. It is in alphabetical order. Main entries are in **dark**, or **bold**, type.

The publisher would like to thank the following for contributing to this book

Photographs
b = bottom, c = centre, l = left, r = right, t = top
Page **12** *tr* Pr S.Cinti/CNRI/SPL, *c* CNRI/SPL, *cl* Pr P.M. Motta & T. Fujita/University "La Sapienza", Rome/SPL, *bc* Pr P.M. Motta & S.Correr/SPL; **13** *bc* SPL; **14** *cl* Martin Dohrn/SPL, *c* Quest/SPL; **15** *tc* Martin Dohrn/SPL, *cr* Richard Wehr/Custom Medical Stock Photo/SPL, *br* SPL; **16–17** Telegraph Colour Library/Mel Yates; **17** *bc* SPL; **18** *cl* Telegraph Colour Library/Michael Krasowitz, *c* Images Colour Library; **18–19** David Scharf/SPL; **20** *cl* Scott Camazine/SPL; **21** *bc* James Stevenson/SPL, *cr* CNRI/SPL; **25** *cr* Pr P. Motta/Dept. of Anatomy/University "La Sapienza", Rome/SPL, *bl* CNRI/SPL; **27** *tr* Philippe Plailly/Eurelois/SPL, *cr* Robbie Jack; **29** *c* Adam Hart-Davis/SPL, *cr* Adam Hart-Davis/SPL, **30** *cl* John Birdsall Photography/Clare Marsh, *br* Martin Dohrn/SPL; **35** *cr* GJLP/SPL, *c* CNRI/SPL; **37** *tl* Liysa King/Image Bank, *cr* Taeke Henstra/Petit Format, *bl* Pascal Brousse/Petit Format; **38** *cl* Wellcome Dept. of Cognitive Neurology/SPL, *tr* Montrel Neuro Institute/McGill University/CNRI/SPL; **38–39** John Warmsley; **39** *bl* Bubbles Photo Library/LoisJoy Thurston; *cr* Tony Stone Images/David Young Wolff; **40** *tl* Hank Morgan/SPL, *tc* Hank Morgan/SPl, *cr* John Greim/SPL, *bc* Will & Deni McIntyre/SPL; **42** *tr* Adam Hart-Davis/SPL, *cr* Adam Hart-Davis/SPL; **43** *tr* Omikron/SPL; **44** *cr* Tony Stone Images/Terry Vine; **47** *tl* Wellcome Trust Medical Photographic Library, *tc* Pr P. Motta/Dept. of Anatomy/University "La Sapienza", Rome, SPL; **49** *cr* Omikron/SPL, *br* (papillae) Prof P. Motta/Dept. of Anatomy/University "La Sapienza", Rome/SPL; **52** *cl* Tony Stone Images/Mary Kate Denny; **54** *bl* Tony Stone Images/Laurence Monneret; **54–55** Tony Stone Images/Doug Armand; **55** *cr* Chris Priest & Mark Clarke/SPL; **56** *cl* SPL; **57** *tl* Tony Stone Iamges/Charles Thatcher, *bl* SPL; **59** *tl* CNRI/SPL, *cr* CNRI/SPL; **60** *c* Damien Lovergrove/SPL, *bl* BSIP, LBL/SPL; **61** Wellcome Trust Medical Photographic Library, **62** *cl* David Scharf/SPL, *br* Petit Format/Malvina Mendil; **62–63** Biology Media/SPL, **64** *cl* Tony Stone Images/Chris Harvey; **65** *cr* J.C. Revy/SPL; **67** *cr* Eddy Gray/SPl, *bc* Collections/Dorothy Burrows; **68** *cl* Damien Lovegrove/SPL, *bc* David Scharf/SPL; **68–69** Matt Meadows, Peter Arnold Inc/SPL; **69** *tl* Yoram Lehmann/Still Pictures, *tr* Matt Meadows, Peter Arnold Inc./SPL, *cr* H.Schleichkorn/Custom Medical Stock Photo/SPL; **71** *cr* Petit Format/J.P. Vidal; **73** *tc* CNRI/SPL; **74** *cl* Dr Klaus Schiller/SPL; **75** *tc* Eye of Science/SPL; **79** *bc* Motta & Familiari/Anatomy Dept./University "La Sapienza", Rome/SPL, *cr* Prof. P.M. Motta G. Macchiarelli, SA Nottola/SPL; **80** *bc* Wellcome Trust Medical Photographic Library; **81** *c* PH Saada/Eurelios/SPL, *cr* Images Photo Library, *bc* Petit Format/Nestle/SPL; **82** *br* Peter Ryan/SPL; **83** Bubbles/ Susanna Price; **84** *cl* Images Colour Library, *c* BSIP Boucharlat/SPL, *bl* Petit Format/Agnes Chaumat; **85** *cr* Images Colour Library, *bc* Images Colour Library, *c* Panos Pictures/Sean Sprague; **86** Biophoto Associates/SPL; **88** *bc* Lawrence Migdale/SPL; **88–89** Mark Edwards/Still Pictures; **89** *tl* Panos Pictures/Mark McEvoy, *tr* Images Colour Library, *cr* Panos Pictures/Sean Sprague, *bl* Panos Pictures/Penny Tweedie; **90** *cl* Tony Stone Images/Frank Siteman, *bl* Tony Stone Images/David Madison; **91** *bl* Tony Stone Images/Donna Day, *cr* Tony Stone Iamges/David Young Wolff; **92–93** Tony Stone Images/John Kelly; **93** *tl* Tony Stone Images/Carin Krasner, *cr* Tony Stone Images/Sara Taylor; **94** *cl* Tony Stone Images/Julian Calder, *bl* Wellcome Trust Medical Photographic Library; **94–95** Tony Stone Images/Mark Harme; **95** *tr* Dept. of Clinical Radiology, Salisbury District Hospital/SPL, *cr* BSIP Laurent/Science Photo Library; **96** *cl* Panos Pictures/Heldur Netocny/Pakistan, *c* Peter Menzel/SPL, Science Pictures Ltd/SPL, *tr* James Stevenson/SPL; **97** *tl* James Stevenson/SPL, *tc* Dept. of Clinical Radiology, Salisbury District Hospital/SPL, *tr* US Department of Energy/SPL, *c* Mehau Kulyk/SPL, *cr* Tony Stone Images/Mary Kate Denny, *bc* Wellcome Trust Medical Photographic Library.

Every effort has been made to trace the copyright holders of the photographs. The publishers apologise for any inconvenience caused.

Additional illustrations
Mike Atkinson, Peter Bull, Robin Carter, Ruth Lindsay, Jonathan Potter, Mike Saunders, Rob Shone, Linda Thursby, Ray Turvey.

Models
Ajay Athwal, Bibbanpreet Bahd, Rajpriya Bahd, Molly Bray, Cristobal Castillo, Brian Cusack, Christopher Davis, Eleanor Davis, Mike Davis, Teresa Davis, Marianne Gingell, Trey Horne, Lucy Jennings, James McMeeken, Jake Marley, Sanjeevan Paramothayan, Gabriel Porter-Tierney, Angelina Sidonio, Dominic Sidonio, Philippa Stroud, William Swart, Alice Wright.